CODEX ARISTARCHUS

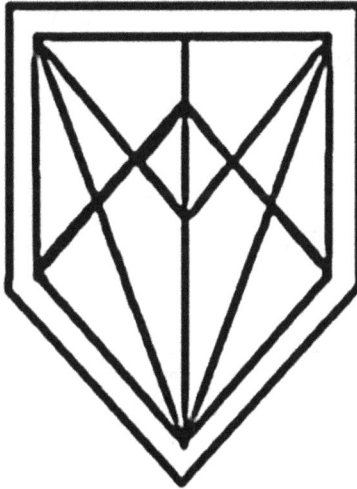

CODEX ARISTARCHUS

Edited by A. A. Morain

Dedicated to the Haunters at the Threshold,

the Ascended Masters

Communio cum aliis Electissimus

Educet me in tenebris inpellentur

Lamia dei

tangunt me cum essentia

commune cum me

Lamia dei, commune cum me

FOREWORD

When vampirism of a legitimate sort, not of the variety beloved by role-players and lifestyle fetishists but rather the kind of a genuinely occult nature, most often circulated and oftentimes only circulated in a very real underground network of adherents, melds with the equally amoral praxises of the Order of the Nine Angles - both patently amoral in spirit and application - a black and sinister alchemy occurs.

The products of this horrifying synthesis are rife with opportunities for both highly blasphemous individual and collective transfiguration through the auspices of the harsh alchemical change process, laden with trauma self-induced, collectively applied within internal discipline (in the most tangible sense of the term) and wrought as well on those unsuspecting - those who have been co-opted, volunteered against their will in one way or the other.

ONA taken as a whole has always promoted that which is predatory and amoral - from the exacting and oftentimes sadistic testing of its own adherents, to the promotion and alleged engagement in human sacrifice up to and including a documented involvement in the promotion - if not outright participation - in terrorism, that greatest and most disruptive heresy of our age.

Wamphyrism applies the premiums on real-world evil, brutal physical training, a life-long sinister questing for a higher platform of physicality and consciousness and a predatory - if selective - outlook as posited by Traditional Satanism and unleashes it, accelerates it - providing a completely and totally amoral outlook, literally beyond human and directly informed by those predatory, interdimensional entities known to Traditional Satanists as the Dark Gods but referred to by those subscribing to the Wamphyric cultus as the Undead - the Ascended Masters.

In *Codex Aristarchus*, A.A. Morain and the central leadership apparatus of the Drakon Covenant - founded in Dark Yorkshire, home to the historic Temple of the Sun, one of the foundational groups who merged with others to become the Order of Nine Angles, an area also renown for the sacrificial pastimes of the Moors Murderers - presents a no holds barred and intensely occult analysis of Wamphyrism, suitable in both content and scope for the readers themselves to step upon the black path of the Undead - a path wreathed in the torment of victims both psychical and fleshly - toward a state beyond human - promising neither the comfort of a right-hand path iteration of paradise nor a cessation of all things, that in itself yet another, perhaps more impersonal future, yet similar, but instead a spectral, ghostly and highly malefic existence suspended between life and death.

In this - as is all things associated with Wamphyrism - there is none of the life-affirming moralism, so solar, so mundanely ordinary, which appeals to the selective adherents of Traditional Satanism and its associated praxises - nor is there the broad strokes of seeming adherence to annihilation, so often cosmetic, beloved by those under the anti-cosmic banner. Instead, not only an exhortation but in fact a pathway - dark and rife with danger as it is - toward an unholy zenith far beyond the horizons forseeable by those in the stages of initiate and, in fact, oftentimes only glimpsed by the adept.

An aspiration toward Wamphyrism is an aspiration toward that which will harm - not only others, whatever their status may be in terms of human society and human relationship - friends, family, associates - man, woman, child - all the same, all equal subjects for predation, exemptions false in designation for the vampire - but harm untold for the self as well and, perhaps, especially so.

For, within Wamphyrism, all that is human must die - immolated in the fires of a hate unnatural and Undead - for the predator to arise. For this path is not for all - and, perhaps, oftentimes not only for some - in that the spirits, once raised, will be most neglectful of showing mercy for those unsuitable and, in exacting, acausal torment, oftentimes even more unmerciful for those who may in fact have that rare and horrific filament of inhuman nature that might allow passage, rife with sorrow, to the land of the dark immortals.

Czar Azag-kala
The Hinterlands
March 24th, 2016

CONTENTS

CODEX ARISTARCHUS

THE VAMPYRIC AIMS OF THE DRAKON COVENANT

In order to sustain itself, a living causal organism – by its very existence in the causal as a causal being composed of causal matter – must obtain causal energy in the form of, for example, carbohydrates. That is, it ingests sustenance – food – and extracts from this matter the type of causal energy required, in whatever form.

However, it is possible to theorize that if a living organism could obtain and in some way use acausal energy itself, it might have no need of such causal matter as sustenance, just as, in theory, such an acquiring of acausal energy could change (that is, make more healthy, and extend) the causal life of such an organism.

–David Myatt, The Philosophy of the Numen

The Drakon Covenant is a small, secretive order of individuals, known to one another who have devoted their lives to the pursuit and attainment of a lichlike existence beyond death (and during life). Our aim is simple: the creation of a vampyric phenotype which can sustain itself on human hosts to haunt this earth and the cold star filled void for as long as we desire. Our primary means of doing this is through the opening of our own nexions, via the exploration of the unconscious, as well as the various methods of astral travel.

We are exploring and are testing, thanks to many dedicants willing to help us, ways in which to feed off the essence of the astral shadows we find, as well as larger hosts such as animals and humans. Our ultimate goal is to transfer our existence into other causal bodies, willing or unwilling, beyond death; or to create a strong enough form to continue existence in the causal/acausal and thus act as teachers to some, horrors to others. Vampyrism, or more precisely astral vampyrism (also known as 'psychic vampyrism') is a method and a practice by which one can feed off the acausal energy of another life form. If the acausal energy of a life form can be said to be that which animates the individual, and death occurs when this acausal connexion wanes and severs, then a supplanting of consciousness within the acausal body (as happens in OBEs and NDEs), and a sustaining of the form via astral feeding may therefore yield a form of immortality. Whether such immortality results in the adept living on as a sort of wraith, or the acausal body is able to inhabit the causal form of another; or the adept is able to move into the acausal regions and create a new form which can presence in the causal, has yet to be tested. Those wishing to participate in this ambitious experiment must know it will require not only a lifetime's work and dedication, but will also require one or more dedicants of a particular empathic skill and affinity with the potential vampyr. The results and outcome are uncertain.

As such, this path is suited only for those truly dedicated to the Sinister path and whom are thus able and willing to ascend to true mastery of the Black Arts. A working knowledge of the acausal should be recognised by the experimenter. Texts such as *The Philosophy of the Numen* and *The Theory of the Acausal* by David W Myatt, as well as ONA MSS such as *The Ontology and Theology of Traditional Satanism* should be studied, among other insightful writings.

This is another reason why the path of vampyrism is really only suited toward adepts. This process is an experimental and experiential one, requiring insight and a certain degree of pathei-mathos. A novice would follow any and all advice, or the wrong advice, and could very well end up a gibbering idiot along with the rest of the failures. Such an existence is certainly not desired.

Vampyrism is the creation of a new type, a new phenotype of Homo Sapiens. As such, we will be above the human in the food chain. Humanity is currently the apex predator, the top dog in evolution. Ascending above them will see us become the ultimate life-form, which lesser humans will come to recognise.

If the practise of post-mortem vampyrism allows causal intrusion and manipulation, we will become revered by those who serve us, those adepts aspiring to vampyric ascension, and with our connection to the acausal, we will possess wisdom which no mortal could ever hope to attain. Thus we will be akin to gods.

A mastery of exteriorisation (astral travel) and familiarity in this form is of absolute necessity to attain a vampyric nature; simply pretending one can feed by touch or sight is a highly subjective belief, and cannot be truly ascertained by the adept, beyond placebo effects. During exteriorisation, one should be able to actually see such feeding occurring. The adept will then become aware of vampyric mechanics and be generally confirmed in their belief that such a process actually occurs. The key to this still growing science is experimentation and cataloguing of phenomena; that is, one is encouraged to deviate from the practises laid out here and elsewhere, to discover suitable methods and results. When more favourable methods and results are found, the adept must be sure to note them down to record such advancements. In this way, the art and science of vampyrism will be progressed and refined, and immortality will in time become a reality for all those who attain Sinister and vampyric mastery.

According to the ONA:

"...the very purpose and meaning of our individual, causal – mortal – lives is to progress, to evolve, toward the acausal, and that this, by virtue of the reality of the acausal itself, means and implies a new type of sinister existence, a new type of being, with this acausal existence

being far removed from – and totally different to – any and every Old Aeon representation, both Occult, non-Occult and "religious". Thus it is that we view our long-term human social and personal evolution as a bringing-into-being of a new type of sinister living, in the causal – on this planet, and elsewhere – and also as a means for us, as individuals of a new sinister causal species, to dwell in both the causal and acausal Universes, while we live, as mortals, and to transcend, after our mortal, causal "death", to live as an acausal being, which acausal being can be currently apprehended, and has been apprehended in the past, as an immortal sinister being of primal Darkness."

The Drakon Covenant strives to do this by achieving what has been termed elsewhere as an 'intercausal existence'; existing in both realms simultaneously in a more overt manner than which we currently do. As star-wraiths, our Imperium will stretch to the farthest reaches of the Cosmos.

We will then be fit to haunt the stars, growing wise beyond reckoning, and feeding eternally upon the human cattle.

Why Vampyrism?

Evolution is an upward increase in consciousness and predation. The ascended entity has the natural right by ability, to utilise prey and make use of the creatures beneath it. That ethics are applied toward the stewardship of those beneath higher entities is honourable and beneficial in regards to ecology; however, in the human issue, a drastic culling is necessary to return the Earth to a natural balance. It is thus logical and a natural progression that an increase in vampyric entities should be engineered.

The vampyr is the natural predator of the profligate human species and whilst intimations of what the vampyric apex predator could be have been in existence for as long as humanity has, it is now time that this phenotype be made a widespread and actual phenomenon.

The chain of Life must continue, and as such, the vampyric aims of the Drakon Covenant will pursued, and the great experiment of Drakon will continue. For those unable to contact and commune with us, publications such as this will be produced so that others may attain true, vampyric mastery.

As for the rest, their fate has been sealed.

Dies Irae.

INTRODUCTION FOR NOVITIATES TO THE ORDER

Novitiates to the Drakon Covenant are to follow the teachings and tasks as given to them by their handler (a vampyric adept), if they are able to find one.

If not, this text shall serve as a guide toward adepthood.

Ordinarily, the novitiate is to serve his/her tutor, assisting him/her in any experiments or tasks they may be pursuing. In return, teachings and advice will be given to aid the novitiate in his/her quest toward adepthood. From there, the adept goes ahead, experiencing the world on their own terms, perhaps in time picking a student of particularly promising character and desire – and thus, the process begins anew.

It is the first task of the novitiate, if not under the tutelage of an adept, to study the teachings of Vampyrism as bequeathed by the Drakon Covenant under the guidance of the current Morain. The Drakon Covenant derives its praxis and ontology in part, from its predecessors, namely the Order of Nine Angles.

The novitiate would thus do well to study the Sinister Tradition for the basic ontology and praxeology with which they will be working. This means:

A working knowledge of the theory of the acausal, the Septenary system – as well as undertaking the hermetic workings as given in the MS *Naos – A Practical Guide to Becoming an Adept,* and *Hostia, Secret Teachings of the ONA,* though one is encouraged to read beyond these two texts – such as the proliferation now available online, as well as classic texts such as Fenrir, Eira and Exeat.

From here, once sufficient ability has been attained (physical, psychological and magickal), true vampyric initiation can begin.

THE RITE OF VAMPYRIC INITIATION

This rite awakens the latent vampyric aspects within the psyche and serves to mark a beginning of the quest toward immortality and true will to power.

A blade or razor is required, as well as parchment or good quality paper, upon which the sigil of the Drakon is to be drawn.

Prior to this, a Black Fast should be observed for one day (a black fast includes the minimal amount of speaking, socialising and the eating of no food, or if eating, then only one light meal – no meat).

Go to a nearby cemetery or graveyard, on the new moon – it is preferable to go when the moon is in Saturn. The more suitable areas are those cemeteries which are old, overgrown and generally have places where you will not be seen. Such places are also home to the shades of the dead, whose spirits linger in such places and whose presence you should ignore during this rite.

Find a suitable spot to sit and meditate for 10-15 minutes on the sigil of Drakon. After this, chant the Diabolus thrice, after which you pick up the parchment and pen and draw the Drakon sigil, whilst vibrating *AGIOS O SATANAS*.

Pick up your razor and incise a cut on your person, applying blood to the parchment whilst saying 'my blood for the quest'.

Burn the parchment over a candle whilst saying 'my gift for the Dark Gods'.

Now stand, with arms outstretched and say 'witness I (your name), begin my quest to become a vampyr! All shall tremble before my Will, seen and unseen denizens of this world! I shall ascend to the throne of Black Immortality and crush all who defy me! Witness now the birth of the Dread One! *AGIOS*!

Now, take a handful of the grave dirt upon the ground and smear it on you. Meditate for a few more minutes before bowing to the North, and leaving.

Following your initiation, each night, before you sleep, visualise as strongly as possible your etheric form departing from your physical, and seeking out a victim, asleep in their bed. You should strive to visualise this act as clearly as possible. You will know you are succeeding when your dreams become more intense or you begin to lucid dream. From here, you should begin to apply the techniques of mastering astral projection.

Further Notes for Novitiates

One real world task for the novitiate would be to infiltrate local 'New Age' and 'pagan' groups or attend fairs of the same. Often these idiots will hold 'wiccan' celebrations, where they will conduct public rites and energy raising rituals. Having prepared yourself beforehand and opened your Blood Centres to draw in sustenance, stand within view and visualise the energy being raised either feeding yourself or being redirected towards a goal you yourself have formulated (perhaps forcing the energy into a preconstructed sigil or striking an enemy). It is best not to draw attention to yourself in these instances, and use such an event as training for your natural shape shifting ability, to move among the masses.

Practise feeding while you are among the crowds; look at a crystal as if you are going to buy it and visualise your hands infusing it with black, vampyric energy that will cause chaos in the life of whoever eventually buys it.

Surely, the zealous vampyr can think of other novel methods with which to cause terror and increase their own power. One method utilised a while back by a Covenant member was to leave a suspect looking suitcase at a Wiccan outdoor workshop, complete with wires displayed. The panic which ensued when the suitcase was discovered added a suitable garnish to the Blood Essence of those whom he fed upon, who gathered in stupoured crowds. The temporary evacuation of the stalls was also an amusing aside, and also provided adequate cover for obtaining a few sizeable chunks of quartz.

There will also arise the opportunity to subvert and convert those more extreme individuals among such groups, for which you should keep an open eye for. It is advised against that you flaunt, even in private, your vampyric pursuits until you are sure your targets are willing to 'go beyond the pale' and truly embrace the path of Drakon. If you fail, all the more experience for you to work on in the future.

DISCIPLINE AND TERROR

The principal directives of the Drakon Covenant are DISCIPLINE and TERROR. To this end, the novitiate should be utterly firm in his/her resolution and commit fanatically to the vampyric path, in spite of the odds.

DISCIPLINE involves honing the will to an obsidian sharp point with which you shall cut through the dross of humanity and carve your name upon the history of this planet. Nothing is too great, too difficult, too terrible for you, the Black Adept in your quest for Power and Wisdom. Discipline is what distinguishes us from the mundane herd. Discipline will guide you to the peaks of experience and ability. Discipline in ourselves, to our cause and to our Covenant.

TERROR involves the utilisation and Infiltration of those groups which seek destabilisation, or have a radically diametric view to the consensus (see *Insight Roles – A Sinister Necessity*). Far right, far left, religious or otherwise – an organisation or movement should be identified, and the vampyric operative should implant themselves firmly within it. Through covert infiltration, you will experience life as a radical, and be forced into certain situations and ordeals which test the character, which build firmness of character – which make the character. All harsh experience – conflict, suffering – all this is fuel to the fire. Manipulation of individuals within these organisations and further radicalisation of the form chosen and the people within it will lead to further conflict, and thus you will be assistant in the Grand Experiment, moving the world further toward a state that we, the Master Elite of the Drakon Covenant, see fit to our purpose. Become a shining example of these twin doctrines, and the world shall be yours.

Are You Tough Enough?

The Drakon Covenant deals extensively and directly with discarnate entities of a wholly vampiric nature. Such entities, whilst capable of bequeathing incredible amounts of knowledge and power, are also extremely malicious and terrifying to encounter – and the resultant delirium brought about by Their dread presence is enough to destroy the feeble minded.

As such, no amount of studying and memorising of chants can prepare the novitiate for Communion with these entities.

The novitiate therefore must be thrust into enacting real world acts of terror and evil. There must be a complete stripping of any safe or sane values still held. One must be made into a predator in the flesh. There is simply no room nor time for flamboyant titles or rituals, nor grades of office. The Drakon Covenant functions more closely to the meaning of a "cult" than most organisations in existence today in that we are not averse to committing very real acts of terror in order to a to achieve our aims. Pragmatically, there is no difference between cursing a foe and breaking into their abode to beat them half to death, leaving little trace of one's forced entry.

All operatives of the Drakon Covenant are therefore forced through a harsh physical regime, which includes combat training with both the fists and weapons. This is not for self-defence, but is simply yet another devotional tool. You will be expected to shed blood – yours and others.

To those able to pass through the crucible of such tests and terror, there is a very esteemed place among our ranks waiting – along with all that entails. For those who falter, the simple act of aligning with us, uttering our chants, hearing our names – that will be enough for us to find you and bind you to our will for as long as we desire.

No mercy, no limits, no fear.

THE MARK OF A TRUE PREDATOR

Much confusion and disinformation surrounds the subject of 'psychic vampirism'. Many self-appointed experts muddy the waters, so to speak, with an intrinsic level of jargon detailing how certain people feed off of emotional states, often talking in very metaphorical terms which shed little light on the subject.

To the more occult oriented aspect of this phenomenon, we see a myriad of idiots expressing a desire to feed due to their perceived 'lack of energy' (what this energy is and what a lack of it means is never really dealt with at length, interestingly). When confronted with the hypocrisy of strictures and rules despite their claims of being predators, they espouse endless humanistic nonsense, performing philosophical somersaults to try and eschew any real acts of evil whilst maintaining their 'dark' persona. No predator assumes the moral outlook of its prey – thus it becomes clear that these 'vampires' are nothing more than just another crowd of mundanes, food for our own kind. Nothing more.

An even more amusing and idiotic theme is that of 'donors'. Of course, among the safe rebellions of Satanism and vampirism, and the asocial, autistic crowds that make up the 'vampire community', such pathetic and parasitical practises are acceptable acts.

The concept of true feeding (which they call 'core feeding' among other names) is almost heresy. Here again we see humans imposing limits on themselves so as not to be brought face to face with their own inadequacies, their own failures, their own inherent inferiority. To those who shirk such qualms however, there is only ever an indulgence in feeding. Nothing beyond this, no grand dreams, no ambition, no wondering just how far this power can be taken.

It is this pathetic motley crew of outcasts that the Ascending vampyric adept will do well to keep a distance from – or perhaps utilise for their own nefarious purposes. It can be safely stated however that of the inner core – the Master Elite that makes up the creative vision of the Drakon Covenant – not a single soul was plucked from the so called 'vampire' community. The potential of this subculture is thin at best. The Vampyric Adept shall cut through such dross as he/she does through the mass of humanity. The mark of a true predator is indiscriminate cruelty.

The path to Vampyric Mastery is not a social one; nor is it a 'fun' path. Ask yourself now if this is really something you are prepared for...

–Agosh Hashallon

MEDITATION IN DEAD STILLNESS

Sit with attention paid toward good posture, still and relaxed yet alert. Now, choose a point in front of you (perhaps a clock face or a symbol or picture on a wall) and gaze at it. Your gaze does not need not be fixed, as this exercise is concerned with bodily stillness and stoic calm among external stimuli.

Do not move. Attain the stillness of a statue. Become like a statue, as calm as the void – totally still. Do this for a minute, adding a minute each time you perform it. It is preferable to practise this once a day. Make use of your time commuting or waiting to master this practise. Be sure to be comfortable in your repose – do not strain yourself unnecessarily.

As you perform this exercise each day, you shall discover a deep sense of patience and calm arising. In the dark, you may notice the subtle energy around you. Vampyrism is concerned with the economy of the acausal Blood Essence that is the life-force; as such, stillness becomes a valuable asset. No more tapping of feet or shuffling out of habit. The grim stillness of Nosferatu now becomes your demeanour. And with it, a noticeable increase in personal reserves of energy.

Become the still, unmoving point of Acausal darkness amidst a sea of chaos and humanity.

THE UNWAVERING EYE

This exercise is designed to hone the ability to fix the gaze at one point for extended periods of time. This ability will become highly useful when learning sight based vampyric feeding. From this, will come a natural ability for the subtle body to feed, especially during astral travel. Thus, this simple practise can be seen as the foundation for all future vampyric practises.

Begin by sitting and staring at a point in front of you (blinking is allowed, naturally).

You will find your eyes tend to wander downward after a short while. If staring at a light wall, spots of colour from your eyes should allow you to see movement of the eyes. For this reason, it is advisable to practise in dim lighting (most, if not all vampyric practises are best performed under the cover of night. This helps create a distinction and is also a useful 'psychic quiet time').

A useful aid in developing this ability is to draw a point on paper, which is then attached to the wall and focus on this point. Novitiates to the Drakon Covenant are often advised to focus on the Drakon sigil, which imparts a two-way flow of acausal energy.

After some time, of a handful of minutes your eyes will create patterns, which you would do well to ignore, as interesting as they may be. All distractions must be cancelled out.

THE ASCENDED VAMPYRIC MASTERS

Those who have risen before us, those who discovered, so many centuries ago, the secrets of Lichood; they lurk ever waiting, feeding upon the masses of human filth who clutter this planet, stalking the astral corridors in collected clans of shrouded darkness.

They wait and watch, and know when they see their own. For that is when they come, and they surely make it known when they do.

The practise of vampyrism, as laid by the Drakon Covenant, *will* in time bring you to the attention of these astral masters. And it is then that your Will is tested, that your Blood Essence shall be sampled, that you will be judged according to your merits.

History has given them many diverse names – Draugr, Sluagh Sidhe, Varkolarkr. What all these cases share in common however is a definite vampyric aspect – something often overlooked in today's obsession with warped and misguided notions of what this entails. In modern times, they have become known as 'Shadow people'.

For as it is written in The Grimoire of Baphomet:

"These other entities are The Dark Daughters of Baphomet, and they – like their Mistress, The Mother of Blood, Baphomet – are thus, in a quite literal sense, beautiful, cultured, alluring but predatory vampires,

whose needed and necessary food is not blood, but rather that acausal energy that animates human beings and makes them alive."

In order to draw the attention of these Undead Masters, and their attendant familiars – and it is communion with them that is the mark of the adept – you have a path strewn with terror and chaos laid before you.

It is *simply not enough* to indulge in vampyric feeding, meditation and the retinue of occult practises to attain the consciousness of Vampyric Metamorphosis. To attract the attention of the Masters via this method alone will surely lead to madness and failure. You must harden your will, make yourself as cold and impersonal as They are. Only then can communion truly take place.

The best way to attain this mindset is through the ordeals and methods offered: insight roles, ritual discipline, indulgence of the taboo (with no limits). Shock yourself, over and over. Read up on the facts of holocaust denial, take a drug you are terrified of, get in a fight, explore an interest you shouldn't. Sleep rough in the woods or the graveyard, but do not lose yourself in the abyss. Remain loyal to your goals, and know when to leave this abyss armed with the hardness of black steel.

Then, your ritual practise of discipline, of vampyric flight; these will attain a further clarity of purpose. And in time, They *will* visit you. See through the terror They bring in their wake, which *will* penetrate every fibre of your being, and learn to put into practise what they *will* teach – if you are worthy.

The presence of Those Who Have Risen is liable to induce panic, despair, and fear of the coldest kind. It is in these moments that the weak among you will capitulate, and call out for God or other such phantoms. God cannot help you here, not now.

Answer me this: if God cannot help the woman who calls out to him while on her knees, the barrel of a terrorist's gun pressed against her head; if God cannot help a young boy who loses his family and home in a monsoon deluge; if God cannot save any of these people who die every day calling out for his mercy, why would he even lift a finger to save you, who has sworn yourself to the endless darkness?

You must learn to harden yourself, toughen yourself, discipline yourself. Your flesh is a piece of iron to be tempered and beaten into shape, to be made strong. Only a strong vessel can hold the Baeldrecan majesty you hope to become.

The Master Elite, the rank and file of the higher echelons of the veritable vampyric Black Lodge move ever closer to the abyss by the day, seeking to become like those Ascended Ones. A direct lineage exists, of a Master Elite, who through their communion with the Ascended Masters (known also as the Undead Gods), bequeath to those below them the teachings of Vampyrism. Through this chain of command, an army of very real, fanatical evil is being equipped and prepared even now as you read these words. The Adepts seek to become like the Masters; the Masters seek to become like the Undead; and you, novitiate, should seek to become like Them also.

Mastery implies a state of being attained which is generally referred to as 'crossing the abyss'. The abyss is that unique region, where the causal and acausal meet, and it is here that a great dissolving of the self takes place. Because of our acausal nature, by virtue of being alive, we all possess the Abyss in a latent form; and magickal development is simply the awakening of this latency, leading to a greater harnessing of this terrible power.

The consciousness can only truly 'pass the Abyss' when it has integrated a unified balance of its causal and acausal aspects. The move toward the Abyss (denoted as Mastery, and which marks our own vampyric Master Elite) signifies a movement of the consciousness into the acausal spaces, or a greater increase of the acausal within the adept. Vampyrism is a unique shortcut to this, though it is not an alternative. The Sevenfold Way must be followed alongside these vampyric pursuits if any glimpse of adepthood is to be attained.

Our Master Elite then are very much the vanguard of the coming Dark Age, the Anarchaeon. And in time, this Master Elite will ascend, as Wamphyri, and become the gods of the New Aeon.

So do not turn to the light when They visit, especially not if you called for Them in the first place. For what is worse? Being subjected to the terrors of Those whom you wish to become like, or being abandoned, left to walk the earth as a mundane, for the rest of your days?

Guide us, oh Unholy ones, into the darkest corners of the night and ascend with us as we become like you, hallowed and eternal.

ASCENDING AS WAMPHYRI

Being a short treatise on the practise of
Astral Travel and Blood Feeding

The Vampyr must feed, in order to harvest more Acausal Blood Essence and ascend the Chain of Being to the pinnacle of black perfection.

Upon what must you feed? The masses of sleeping humanity.

The following is an instructional guide utilised by the Drakon Covenant to achieve vampyric flight in the astral. The method has been proven to work effectively. The technique comes in two parts – energy raising and exteriorisation. Focus upon the acausal energy and its introduction to the primary Blood Centres constitutes the main work of the first part. Exiting the body through a specific technique is dealt with in the second part.

Part I

Begin by laying down and focussing attention to your breath. Follow it passively as it flows in and flows out. Do this for a few minutes until you feel content and your mind is clear. With the regular practise of the novitiate exercises, this should not be too difficult.

Now, begin to feel your descent into the Abyss with each external breath – like you are sinking in a black ocean of infinite depth, one tiny point in a vast darkness. This is a useful method to induce a deep state and shift to Alpha brainwave functioning.

Do this until your mind is clear and you feel relaxed.

Next visualise the sigil of Drakon above you, raining down Blood Essence, crimson-violet in colour with filaments of plasma arcing through it. As you breathe in, this Blood Essence bathes you and fills your being, clearing tension from you on the outward breath.

Now visualise the Blood Essence around you being pulled through your feet to the first Blood Centre, opening it and infusing it with energy. Then pull energy through your feet again to the next energy centre until all are complete (For further information on the Blood Centres, see below).

Abide in this deep state for a few minutes if you wish.

Part II

Now visualise a black Tendril descending from the Drakon Sigil, and with your astral hands, grasp it. Pull yourself up out of your body using the Tendril, and keep focusing on this until you feel yourself begin to detach from your body.

This Blood Essence is channelled Acausal energy, made manifest via the use of a numinous symbol (in this case, the Drakon Sigil). The Vampyric aspect of the working triggers your unconscious into a predatory mind-set, thus making it much easier to project in the future. This is so because the unconscious will come to associate projecting with feeding, and the unconscious connection to the lower brains/instincts will naturally yearn to feed, these lower instincts being concerned primarily with feeding and survival.

In this way, one can subtly condition their being to project much more efficiently and in a manner fit for a Vampyric Adept.

You may find this difficult at first. It is often noted that a deep state often occurs around the time you focus on pulling up through the rope/tendril. If this is the case, repeat the procedure upon entering a deep state. You will know this state because your breathing will become semi-automatic, similar to when sleeping.

Upon success of this method (which may take numerous tries or may work instantly), explore your surroundings and become familiar with travel in this form.

Of course, this technique is rather complex in its many parts. As such, it should be utilised preferably once a day, optimally before sleep. After performing this, imagine your astral body leaving your physical and flying into the night, just before you settle to sleep. A recommended adaptation is to practise part I one night, followed by part II the next, until you feel satisfied with the results.

Such prolonged visualisation can be mentally exhausting, and thus it is recommended that certain tasks (such as ascending the tendril, taking in the Blood Essence) be done using tactile imaging – that is, psychically 'feeling' these acts as opposed to 'seeing' them in your mind's eye. This subtle technique will be known to those who master psychic abilities.

You will notice this exercise increases the vividness of your dreams, which will point to success.

Then, when you are ready to astral project at will, simply relax into the trance state through breath exercises and employ the tendril technique. From here, persistence and experimentation are your best pointers toward attaining astral flight.

As an aid toward the methods outlined pertaining to Vampyric Flight, the following exercise should be observed strictly.

Each night, you are to set an alarm for 3 am. You may wash or have a light meal, or do some light exercise before chanting the Diabolus. Then settle back into bed and visualise the tendril and your astral hands climbing it as outlined earlier. This is to be performed for a week – and from then on performed alternately every week (that is, adhered to every night for one week, then left for week, the resumed again for a week and so on until success).

The break up in your nightly sleep cycle, while only minimal, will help you adjust to hypnagogic states and bring about lucidity much quicker.

The flowing of energy through the body, beginning at the feet, and the opening of the Blood Centres can be performed as a standalone meditation in itself, and should be practised at least twice a week.

A modification of the Tendril aspect of the rite involves opening the Blood Centres and visualising the Drakon sigil extending a tendril into your solar plexus and siphoning acausal energy into your core. This is a useful energy raising meditation and should be used in conjunction to ascertain effects.

<u>A Note on the Blood Centres</u>

The Blood Centres are specific energy points situated along the body which regulate the flow of acausal energy. These are seven in number, and their main use of concern to the Vampyric is in their role as energy accumulators for the astral body. They have many names, most notably Chakras, from the Sanskrit Vedic tradition in which they are written about explicitly).

The Blood Centre locations are as follows:

The perineum

The sacral region

The solar plexus

The heart

The centre of the throat

Between the eyes

Atop the head – at the crown

Within the Vampyric tradition, these centres are utilised primarily for infusing the subtle body with acausal Blood Essence, thus increasing the practitioners' acausal charge and yielding greater results during Vampyric Flight.

Much can be learnt from studying Vedic and Eastern texts which deal with these energy centres. In the praxis of the Drakon Covenant, they shall be dealt with purely as they are – devoid of the mysticism and dogma of the New Age fads.

Further practises and techniques are readily available via Covenant leadership, as well as auxiliary texts yet to be produced. These should be pursued only after the above techniques are mastered.

REVOLUTION AND TERROR

The Master Elite demand power be exercised at all levels, from bottom to top, from within to without; all directives of the Drakon Covenant, and by that extension, the immaculate, unquestionable word of the Ascended Masters, is to be enacted without fail by the vampyric militants that make up our order, wherever they may be throughout this globe.

A ruthless and calculating mindset needs to be cultivated – and the diabolical taint that will be brought via the touch of the Ascended Masters will most certainly help you in developing such.

The Vampyric fanatic must be embedded within disruptive elements, whether they be centred on themselves (in the form of creating antagonistic political groups, criminal enterprises or cult like followings) or centred elsewhere (in the form of joining antagonistic political groups, criminal enterprises or cult like followings). Of these three, political insurrection is the most likely to presence change on a real level. Of this, Fascism is the most likely to emerge in the current era, as well as possessing the most commonality of belief with the teachings outlined by the Master Elite.

Mirrored with this must be a relentless pursuit of acausal shock tactics: the rite of Communion must be sought without hesitation, as well the fine tuning of the energy body in preparation for your forays as a terrifying predator – all these must be practised alongside physical ordeals aimed at hardening the body.

To this end, the Vampyric initiate must learn to view the mind and body as separate, distinct entities. The body is the vessel of the Will, created to presence this Will upon the realm of phenomena, the arena of evolution.

The physical vessel must then be conditioned, via physical feats of endurance and strength. Ritual flagellation must be indulged in with zeal, combined with the chants of the Diabolus and the Communio. Sinister Chant must be practised upon lonely peaks and regions, having exerted the self physically arriving at such places.

This recreation of the individual self must be conspired so as to reflect within society. The subversion of the existing order and a replacement with a new order is a necessity. You must place yourself within those movements which hold promise of election and power, so long as they radically differ from the current status quo, within which the vampyric worldview would never find prominence.

One example of how such an occult manoeuvre was orchestrated can be seen within the NSDAP under Adolf Hitler. The Thule Society was but one involved factor which saw Hitler's rise to power. They were a collaboration of Volkisch supporters interested in promoting their trades and efforts toward a greater Germany. Many of these had mystical and neo-pagan beliefs. These, and individuals such as Heinrich Himmler and Rudolf Hess, saw to it that the Third Reich would be an embodiment of pagan order, and we see the adoption of Germanic runes, of ritual practises of the SS, and of a mystical understanding of Blood and Soil.

We will see society becoming unrecognisable over the next century, as racial conflict and tribal degeneration continue. Despite all the smug urbanite claims of moving toward a progressive, global community, the Magians have gotten it all wrong: existence is the will to power, and differing agencies all want power. In allowing them to grow unchecked, in forcing them to intermingle, the Magian house of cards is going to come toppling down, and at this point, the revolutionaries must seize power, with the servants of the Undead Gods hidden amidst their ranks. Only then will we have a direct chain of command, a hierarchy fit for the coming Anarchaeon. And when we have emerged from such a dark age, we will have restructured the entire human species toward further evolution, order and greatness.

Individualism vs. Unity

How often do we see the endless myriad of ineffective cults and 'temples' spew their rhetoric of 'granting power to the individual' of giving the 'individual power over their destiny', and endless paeans to the supposed power of individuality This half-hearted rebellion against the collectivism we see in society today is the primary reason such cults never make it past the minds of their handful of deluded followers. All of the power structures we see today exist because they know that the individual is nothing compared to the combined power of a collective. The 'destiny of the individual' is nothing compared to the unity of vision, imposed from above upon a willing and select few. It is for this reason that the greatest shapers of human destiny have NOT been these temples, and has in fact been movements such as religion, Socialism, Fascism and so on.

Understand this: The Undead Gods do not want a 'free and empowered individual'; they want a dedicated and amoral bastard, hardened and aware of his/her place in the world, with a ruthless desire to conquer and overcome. To succeed, you must understand the chain of command. You must understand that everything you are taught herein comes directly from bitter experience and often soaked in the blood of those who were at the sharp end of such learning via experience.

Only then, will you be aware of your place within something greater, of which you benefit from the collected wisdom of those who have gone before.

We look forward to a day when the ranks of the Master Elite greet the return of the Ascended Masters and the Dark Gods, who will grant us knowledge and power to conquer the cold, star filled void of space, and spread a new epoch among the galaxy. Our aim is unflinching and uncompromising – either you are with us or you are against us.

The entire arena of human existence will be placed beneath our Will, and utilised so as to craft the species into an indomitable, black convergence of Discipline and Terror.

Do you understand yet what is demanded of you? Can your body withstand such punishment? Can your mind withstand such stress?

Can you be a shining black example of the Vampyric to those around you?

Crush all who stand before you. Do not fail the Dark Gods – for that is a far worse fate to bear.

"If you want a vision of the future, imagine a boot stamping on a human face – forever."

–1984

THE SEVENFOLD WAY AND VAMPYRISM

The genuine Western Tradition had its genesis in Ancient Greece and it is from this tradition which all true adepts of the past have drawn from – long before the introduction of the garbled Jewish Qabalah of which so much modern magick is based upon.

To this Western tradition, there is no casting of circles, no words of power, no banishing rituals, no godforms, no endless and pointless correspondences which bear little semblance to reality. There is simply the individual, and an understanding that he/she is a Gate – a *nexion* to the acausal. This acausal energy is around us in every living species, and waxes and wanes in certain parts of the Earth, which is itself a type of living organism.

From this Western Tradition, we derive the methods of adeptship and apply them to the praxis of vampirism, which has a history and tradition equally as ancient and efficacious.

As outlined in the ONA MS *Naos*, the pathways and spheres can be seen as regions of acausal energy within the psyche, as well as specific gates to accessing this energy. Apprehension of this energy moves us away from unconscious knowing to conscious understanding – a harnessing of these energies and thus a greater increase in acausal energy. And from there, evolution proper.

Vampyrism deals specifically with the taking of this acausal energy from other living beings, as the Natural order implies. All living beings feed upon one another. The vampyr is an apex predator, and His/Her prey is the human race, long regarded as the peak of Nature's evolutionary food chain. How very wrong.

From this feeding and accumulation of energy, we arrive at a state only fables now recall, but a practise which has seen forays from the ancient Germanic tales to the far away Egyptians. This state is the natural consequence and ultimate goal of the vampyric adept – Lichood.

However, as stated, simple Vampyric feeding is no substitute for an initiated apprehension of Acausal energy. All the feeding in the world will not shed light on those unexplored regions of the psyche, represented and guarded by the Dark Gods. For such apprehension, and thence a move toward adepthood, the pathways, spheres and grade rituals must be followed through. Whilst these are enacted via a specific vector (that of Drakon Covenant brand vampyrism) the core essence remains the same, though understood in a more terrible aspect. There still remains, after such practises and gnosis, a deeper understanding of Acausal energy and the cosmos and the Self as a whole

Many trials and ordeals lay between the initiate and the state of the Undead Lich, a path strewn with the blood and despair of all who cross you.

Go now, and build your empire, your legacy – your pyramid of skulls.

LAMIA NATURALIS

There are, and always have been, those few individuals whom are naturally adept in the methods and practise of astral travel and who have sometimes been brought to the attention of the Ascended Masters because of such abilities. These few individuals, possessed of a natural skill to leave the physical body with no prior training are referred to as Lamia Naturalis. These rare characters hold vast potential – often they are quite young, and have been known to master the vampyric arts and attain Communion far swifter than the average novitiate.

Often, these individuals (by virtue of their accumulated Acausal charge) were the targets of poltergeist-like activity and vampyric entities, which coalesced and fed upon such unfortunate victims. Thus, their lives were marked by a frequency of night terrors, disease and affliction. Their change would often be noticed by superstitious parents, who referred to them in past times as 'changelings', and from there the folk superstition that these children had been replaced with faery folk took root. Some stories tell of changelings who forget their faery origin and thus go about living a rather normal human life – with the exception of their natural powers, for which they are praised or hated, according to the custom of the times. Celtic and Nordic legends abound with such figures, and the name Siofra, a popular Irish girl's name, means elf or changeling.

What truth there is to this legend is unknown. But that a sort of change did occur is confirmed – a death of the astral form and a replacement with a malign vampyric entity. This process is known as Kenosis-Demonosis, and the unwitting victim thus becomes a very real Lamia Naturalis in this case, albeit an unwilling one.

There is an ability to master this power consciously however, given the correct guidance and understanding. This in no way detracts from the severity of such a venture; and whilst very real possession is not an uncommon occurrence among vampyric initiates and adepts alike, the permanent indwelling of a host by an astral vampire is an abhorric manifestation nevertheless.

And it is this ultimate aim which the Vampyric master strives toward.

The Rite of Transference

According to tradition, a vampyric black lodge was headed by a Master (referred to as a Morain, or Moraina if female) and his/her retinue of trusted confidants, whom he/she had schooled in the black arts, and whom had attained adeptship. Upon entering close to the point of death, the Master would elect one of his adepts to take his/her place, this individual having being prepared and trained in private by the Master for some time prior.

Following this, the Master would address their final few affairs before retreating into solitude. Some Masters were rumoured to have sought to extend their life via scientific methods (one infamous example being the Blood Tank); others ended their existence with a suicidal takedown of the lodge's enemies, or a pertinent mundane figure. Others still followed an ambitious rite, the ultimate black pact. This was known as the Rite of Transference.

The Rite involves a host, who has offered to give up their conscious life (or a pre-identified Lamia Naturalis, whom would preferably be unaware of the lodge's interest in him/her, though often a lodge member was groomed years or months in advance for this honour). The Master then ascends into the astral and enters the body of the willing host. This was usually done with a ritual sacrifice of the Master upon his/her astral ascent, and the host would either direct their essence toward the Master, or into a crystal. Braver souls offered their services to the Ascended Masters who would usher them away to the darkest astral corners.

A fast and other various horrific disciplines were observed by the lodge leading up to this Rite, with the host in particular enduring heroic feats of self-torture so as to induce a catatonic separation of mind and body.

Following completion of this Rite, the host would be questioned so as to ascertain success on the Master's part.

Another variant of this Rite was for the Master to enter into the body of a new-born or unborn child, who would then be raised within the care of the lodge, who would name the child by his/her former name, and in time hope to bring the child to recall its previous life. This continuation of consciousness within a specific physical parameter is but one way in which the tradition and teachings were preserved through harsher times, when adepts of all pursuits were under heavy persecution by the Nazarene church. The traditional title of Morain, (meaning *'great'* or *'dreadful'* in the Celtic tongue) was passed down to each head of the vampyric lodges, the title rumoured to have originally been the actual name of the first vampyric master to successfully attain Transference. The epithet is used nowadays in the same vein as the Roman usage of the title Caesar, as both a name and title.

Other methods involved the fostering of a bond with certain astral entities, or for those more self-assured, the burial of their remains within the grounds of their ritual space (often an isolated cottage or forest).

In modern times, the liberal outlook has fostered a general disbelief in such practises, if only outwardly. And thus, the grand experiment of the Black lodges and the Drakon Covenant may resume, unhindered.

Sigil of the Morain

THE WAMPHYRIC TENDRIL

The Wamphyric tendril is the next aspect of the Metamorphic cycle to focus upon. This should be practised consistently throughout the day, among the crowded streets and places people frequent. The mastering of the Wamphyric tendril should be practised alongside your astral forays.

Skill in conjuring the tendril lies in two direct methods;

1) The concentration and visual discipline obtained through practises such as the Unwavering Eye and image focus
2) Training the subtle body to act in a certain manner via repetition of visualisation

The tendril is the primary 'organ' which you must develop in order to feed on the Blood Essence of your victims. This tendril exists in all humans, in nascent form. It has been noticed that certain people, close to dying will drain those around them, inexplicably wearing them down to the point of extreme fatigue. This is the astral tendril reaching out unconsciously and feeding on the nearest source, so as to prolong the person's life.

The use of the Wamphyric tendril is subtle and simple. It relies on the skill you gain from the Unwavering Eye and Dead Stillness.

Select a suitable victim (you must never substitute a victim with a 'donor'; this is highly advised against. Feeding, especially in its more adept cases, can lead to extreme debilitation and death. It also nullifies the necessary predatory instinct needed to further awaken this aspect of the self. Experimentation is recommended, however – especially with useful acolytes willing to serve as donors for practise, and upon whom certain disciplinary procedures may be enacted to solicit a generous flow of Blood Essence, astral and physical. But the technique must never be substituted with willing victims).

Upon selecting a victim – whether it be a stranger sat next to you, in front of you or simply near you in public – focus on your core region and visualise the Wamphyric tendril emerging forth, and moving toward your target, where it pierces through their aura. Basking in the Blood Essence, the tendril absorbs it as you inhale, transferring the energy to yourself. Feel it permeate and invigorate upon exhaling. Do this for as long as you feel necessary. Experiment with different time lengths and distances.

Upon completion of feeding, withdraw the tendril and bask in the enhanced energy levels you have just accumulated.

In the beginning, sight contact is necessary – the infamous 'evil eye'. After attaining a sufficient mastery of this technique however, feeding may become possible without the need to keep your eye focused upon your victim.

Some signs that Vampyric feeding is working are:

- Feeling an influx of energy

- Feeling giddy, euphoric and/or light headed
- Feeling heavy and drowsy, or needing to sleep

This practise of feeding must be indulged in often, especially in the early days, when you are first exercising this new organ. As frequent as possible, even hourly – to this end, you should take to travelling to the town or city centre where you live to feed on the masses, taking care so as not to act noticeably.

Following frequent use of the Wamphyric tendril, you may find the visualisation becomes much easier, almost unconsciously willed as the tendril becomes more pliable to your will and stronger in its purpose.

Wamphyric Feeding – Further Notes

To the adept who has attracted the attention of the Undead Masters, there are many methods he/she will be taught in regards to Blood Feeding and other useful practises.

One method which has been bequeathed to the Drakon Covenant is the practise of astral flaying. This involves the usual procedure of Feeding, but utilising the Wamphyric Tendril to tear through the target's aura, to wreck their energy body, akin to a predator tearing open its prey to access the sweet blood within. Tear open the target's energy body, the Blood Centres, thrust through to the core and drink deeply whilst they astrally bleed out. This of course, will lead to potentially severe harm to the target, manifest in many physical ailments as seen in traditional vampyric folk tales. This of course is of no concern to you.

INSIGHT ROLES – A SINISTER NECESSITY

It is often said by Initiates of the Seven Fold Way that of all the physical tasks, the prospects of culling, the numerous difficult tasks, it is insight roles which terrify them the most.

For this reason, they should be pursued even more fervently.

The main issue with Insight Roles is that they are so disruptive to the Initiate's life. This is precisely what they are meant to be, however. Perhaps one fills with dread at the prospect of become a neo-Nazi or a devout Muslim, wondering what one's friends, peers and/or family will think. A suitable answer to this is – if you are living according to the expectations of others, you are not worthy of the fruits of the Sinister path.

Insight Roles are the alchemical process which changes the initiate completely, irrevocably, for the better. Only through these tasks, and the pathei-mathos wrought from such tasks is that unique Sinister nature of the adept formed.

The principal Insight Roles given by the Order of Nine Angles are:

- "Either by foot or by bicycle or by accepting lifts, travel alone around the world, taking between six months to one year (or more). You must live frugally, and carry with you most of what you need. You should travel to as many countries as possible, the more remote the better and expect sometimes to find work to enable you to travel further.

- Become a professional burglar, targeting only victims who have revealed themselves to be suitable (e.g. by testing them – qv. the Order MSS dealing with victims etc.). The aim is to specialize in a particular area – e.g. Fine Art, jewellery – and become an 'expert' in that area and in the techniques needed to gain items.

- Undertake the role-of extreme political activist and so champion heretical views (by, e.g. becoming involved in extreme Right-Wing activism). The aim is to express fanaticism in action and bee seen by all 'right-thinking people' as an extremist, and a dangerous one.

- Become a devout Jihadist Muslim, championing extremist Islamic thinkers and groups.

- Join the Police Force (assuming you meet the requirements) and so experience life at 'the sharp end' and being a servant of a higher authority.

All roles should last for at least six months and all must be completed (i.e. you leave them) before the end of eighteen months. All the roles will by their very nature test your

Satanic Views and beliefs and thus your desire to continue along the sinister way. All will expose you to difficulties.

Once the choice is made, it is up to you to find means of undertaking the role – e.g. in the case of joining the Police, finding reasons why which will convince a selection panel; in the case of becoming a burglar, finding someone to buy your stolen items and so on. The essence of these Insight Roles can be succinctly stated: Incipit Vitriol."

   – *Hostia*

An insight role should last at least 6 months. Certain roles may take much longer (particularly those suited to an Aeonic agenda). And of course, the nature of the insight role should be one which challenges the individual – that is, it exercises the qualities of the individual which have, until now, been generally disregarded. For example, a lazy, criminally inclined individual could expect to join the police force or the military. An excessive hedonist could be expected to join a Buddhist monastery – and so on.

The furthering of Aeonic goals lies in the subtle manipulation of forms chosen, and in this the study of Aeonic magick will be of substantial benefit. For example, as related in the TOB MS, *The Focus and Direction of The Tempel ov Blood*:

"...the infiltration and manipulation of organizations and forms with Sinister potential. Aryanism, particularly the more religiously fanatically forms of it, such as Christian Identity are a good example. The manipulating Noctulian is to use these forms for their own Presencing of the Dark, as well as changing in subtle ways the followers of such forms to following a more Sinister direction.

For example, in Identity, using knowledge of the Biblical doctrines and prophecies encourage war, hardship, and system disruption using the scriptures as guidance and proof of the message you are sending to adherents of the said form. Any form with a transhuman, system disruption, or satanic direction to it may be of use here. The key is finding a form that in itself is an aid to the Dialect and empowering it further, causing a saturation of Acausal Energy."

Those with sufficient insight should be able to survey the current climate of the society they live in and select a role accordingly. Of particular potential at the time and location of writing (126yf, England), those forms useful are Islamic sects, particularly those of a more fanatic bent; the numerous Hare Krishna cults (and among these it may be said, the ambitious operative will find much potential for Sinister manipulation), Hindu nationalist organisations; National Socialist movements (of which England is currently seeing a renaissance); mercenary groups based in mainland Europe; Far Left organisations, particularly those owing allegiance to the more radical sects of Socialism, such as the DPRK or the Khmer Rouge; Animal Liberation and Environmental activists, among whom one will find quite militant personalities. Even better, set up your own cell, specialising in secretly producing propaganda and 'direct action'.

In all these endeavours, a search through the various clandestine corners of the internet should reveal potential forms and ways in which to contact these forms. In pursuit of these roles, one must adopt a fanatical mind-set; an intense study of the relevant material, a contribution to the philosophy/ies of the movements involved – all the while veering them toward more Sinister application. It must never become known to those around you that you are following the 7FW or that you are affiliated with the Order. Revelation of such details should be regarded as failure. The true adept is a shapeshifter; whose real motives are invisible to all around him or her.

This is a basic tenet which needs to be understood.

Always remember to approach these groups with sincerity; it should appear you are simply a curious individual looking to find answers in life or make a change in the world. And remember also to have fun!

It is in posterity that future generations will see the efforts made via the various insight role, and lend infamy among the Sinister and Mundane sphere alike.

Until then, work in secret and work for Them.

ACAUSAL AND ASTRAL VAMPYRISM – THE NECESSARY DIFFERENCE

The fundamental difference lies in the source of energy taken.

The 'aura' of the target is simply a natural response to causal existence by the acausal body. This astral shell shields the individual, absorbing much of the subtle energy relayed to it. Under special circumstances, this aura can be excited and made into a promising food source via the infliction of pain and terror upon the individual – though such practises are beyond the scope of this text.

The true energy lies within the individual. This is their acausal energy, their very Blood Essence. This then, marks the pale imitations from the true vampyrs. Acausal vampirism yields power, can kill and inevitably leads to vampyric metamorphosis. Everything else is merely astral scavenging, akin to feeding upon the garbage of others.

Know then, when feeding during your nocturnal odysseys that the Blood Essence lies behind the astral shell. Tear through and drink deeply.

Acausal Energy and Lichood

A focused conservation and accumulation of energy by the Vampyric practitioner on all levels is necessary for multiple reasons.

The very act of practising magickal rites and of altering one's state of consciousness through such rites opens the gates to the acausal within the self, illuminating aspects of the psyche, which is simultaneously a part of the adepts' mind and the acausal itself. Illumination of these hidden aspects leads to an increase in conscious understanding of Acausal energy and of the self, as well as an actual increase in Acausal energy present within the Adept. This is Vampyric Metamorphosis.

This raising of the acausal charge is the esoteric function behind the process of evolution, and as such, the Vampyric Adept is evolution in motion. This permanent increase is most necessary to attain Lichood, lest the subtle body simply fade away into ever finer dimensions upon the death of the physical form. All living beings possess acausal energy, and the human species is unique in possessing a higher degree than other creatures on this planet. It is because of this lower level of acausal charge that we see very few ghosts/spirits/shades etc. of animals, in contrast to the number of human ghost sightings which are reported.

The next step above the human, in terms of evolution viewed from an acausal energetic perspective (which is the root cause and ultimate objective perspective) is the Vampyric entity. Countless individuals have reported, since time immemorial, of dark beings feeding on them whilst they lay, paralysed in the dead of night. These night terrors, which modern thought refers to as 'sleep paralysis' is simply a natural part of the predatory order. That an increase in encounters over the past century or so – as epitomised by the 'shadow people' phenomena – has been observed is an interesting development and no doubt follows an increase in the functioning and growth of various Vampyric temples and orders.

The Vampyric entity exists in two forms. The first is that of adepts and sorcerers who have developed a high degree of Acausal charge and control of the energy body and upon death, fully realised in his/her ability and nature (whether through being schooled by the Ascended Masters, or perhaps through learned studying) has taken to feeding upon the Blood Essence of living beings to sustain their existence. This may be a simple instinct, a survival mechanism ironically perpetuating the Adept in this post mortem state, or it may be wilfully engaged in, so as to prolong the adepts' existence for his/her own reasons to desire.

The second form is those who have died, under circumstances which have caused their astral form to linger on and refuse to acknowledge death. We see this phenomenon in poltergeist activity, and there are some of these shades who chance upon the ability to feed so as to prolong their state. Often, the inducing of fear and terror in the victims ensures a suitable energetic flow, and this any explain the numerous cases of malevolent spirits and ghosts, though of course, not all spirits exhibit Vampyric behaviour.

The difference between the two forms is that the former willed this state into existence and has retained a modicum of conscious awareness of who they are/were – whereas the latter is often not conscious or aware of the Vampyric aspect of their existence or what potential such an existence possesses.

THE IRRELEVANCY OF CONVENTIONAL MORALITY WITHIN VAMPYRISM

Many texts, books and 'orders' abound, promoting the vampyric path – often with very little insight or experience to give depth to such teachings.

One particular aspect is in the notion of harm and murder. We see endless rhetoric about these vampyric individuals being 'unashamed predators', and recognising that 'survival is the most important law in life'. Yet, they are quick to emphatically state that no harm should be done to a human, or that being a vampyr 'forbids' such acts. That these individuals should profess a belief in the hierarchy of Nature, as well as the supremacy of Vampyrs, yet assert an essentially egalitarian morality clearly shows their lack of understanding. That they assert the belief that vampyrism can indeed take the life of an individual yet claim that intentional harming of a person via physical means is somehow wrong shows their innate disbelief in their own teachings.

Such individuals are best ignored.

The unique praxeology of the Drakon Covenant demands that the vampyric novitiate marry their occult forays with acts of real world evil; acts which most societies deem abhorrent at best, and thoroughly illegal at worst. So many occultists play at being adepts, becoming pale imitations of the powerful and feared black warlocks of yesteryear. There are many excuses the novitiate could make, the principal one being that crime will invariably lead to imprisonment, which would be counter to the vampyr's pursuit of power.

Nothing could be further from the truth.

If you were a seeker of occult secrets, with access to the astral via vampyric flight, would not the best place to reside be behind large, re-enforced walls, where your views and practises would not be subject to scrutiny? Where every day could be spent in solitude, studying and refining one's occult abilities? Where an endless supply of humans exists on all sides, for you to feed on during astral flight?

Despite the mundane claims otherwise, prison is perhaps one of the most fitting places for a would-be vampyr – if indeed only for the metamorphosis which may come about via prolonged solitude and self-reflection.

The question of crime in general however, should be made clear. Crime is a means, not an end. The system and society you live in has created you from the day you were born. Forget now any arrogant and misplaced notions of self-determination and independent thought. Up until now, until your discovery of the Black Arts (in the truest sense of the term), you have thought in terms of abstractions crafted by the system. You have followed trends, upheld ideologies, indulged in past times – all put in place to stop you doing exactly what you are doing right now: discovering your POTENTIAL AND DESTINY.

With this knowledge in mind, the fact that this system deems some acts outside the sphere of 'acceptability' is utterly irrelevant. And as you advance along the path of vampyric metamorphosis and your skills in every sector are enhanced, your ability to enchant people, to find those who would serve well as thralls shall lead you to new heights of liberation, wherein you shall be provided with the tools you need, legally or otherwise.

But always remember: crime is a means, not an end.

SUFFERING FOR THEM – DISCIPLINE PROCEDURES AND RITES

Purchase or fashion an implement suitable for flagellation. Flails of various design are usually best. Do not pick a soft piece of equipment, the type seen among many safe 'BDSM' outlets. If this is the only option available, the item can be modified (usually by tying knots in the tails of the flail).

Sit comfortably or kneel, before the altar of Drakon, upon which should be various items, including the symbol of Drakon, as well as other imagery and paraphernalia suitable to vampyric and totalitarian worship.

Begin the ritual flagellation, whilst chanting the Diabolus, followed by the Communio, three times each.

The Diabolus

Dies Irae, Dies Illa

Solvet Saeclum in Favilla

Teste Satan cum Sybilla

Quantos Tremor est Futurus

Quando Vindex est Venturue

Cuncta Stricte Disscusurus

The Communio

Communio cum aliis Electissimus

Educet me in tenebris inpellentur

Lamia dei

tangunt me cum essentia

commune cum me

Lamia dei, commune cum me

This rite can serve as a suitable prepatory aid for inducing a trance state when combined with preliminary breath exercises and meditation, as well as providing an astral signal to draw near to you the Ascended Masters.

This rite was usually demanded of the novitiate, alongside his/her attempts at astral flight – the rite usually being performed within a cemetery at night, with a notebook nearby to practise automatic writing and thus gain further guidance from Without. The traditional locale for this, during the Drakon Covenant's early days was the Beckett Street cemetery in Leeds, which was situated opposite a workhouse, now known as Thackeray Medical Museum. Both the museum and the cemetery have a legendary history of being haunted (the cemetery possessing numerous mass graves from injuries and accidents occurring at the workhouse).

Other useful practises involve the collecting of sharp implements, such as razors to elicit bloodletting, which can be left in a small bowl upon your altar as an offering to the Ascended Masters, along with incense (frankincense being a particular choice).

Bloodletting and flagellation should be practised with abandon, regularly defiling and harming yourself whilst attempting to commune with the Masters. Only at such fevered heights, and with the correct chants, will They hear you and take notice.

UNDEAD CONFRONTATION – IMPLICATIONS FOR THE ADEPT

As the Vampyric adept moves toward the attainment and cultivation of a truly Sinister retinue of skills and mastery of communion with the Undead Gods, ever more fanatic levels of bravery and dedication are needed.

In the beginning, the novitiate is eager and keen to attain communion, and will enact the necessary chants and rituals to draw the attention of forces which he/she has yet to comprehend.

However, as one achieves such an honor, the sheer horror of Their intrusion into the novitiate's life will take its toll and will be made very real. As physical marks appear on one's body as well as in one's dwelling, and as one's sanity is stripped by night terrors and waking hallucinations, it becomes clear just how deep one has gotten themselves involved.

Because of this, the adept enters into communion with a level of cold fear of which the novitiate has yet to experience. The adept knows fully well just how terrifying these encounters can be.

For this reason, ever heightening levels of discipline and terror are needed, or else the vampyric adept will simply cease and return to their fearful, mundane existence.

The methods outlined by the Drakon Covenant need to be followed out precisely. Just as necessary warm ups – no matter how tiresome or painful – need to be followed in preparation for any physically tasking act, so too do the regimes need to be followed to the letter.

Insight roles, physical trials, acts of amorality and real world evil, manipulation of people and forms – you MUST follow through, or else you will be unfit for dealing with Their presence.

The ensuing onslaught of sleep paralysis, involuntary astral travel and general chaos and dread which mark the successful achievement of Undead contact will tax the adept.

Make no mistake – The Undead Gods are not your friends. Simply serving Them does not mark you out as worthy of special treatment. In fact, the opposite will occur. But this confrontation is something you need to really prepare yourself for. Otherwise, the fast track to Adeptship will pass you by, leaving you wallowing on this planet with the rest of the human dross.

And having come so far, is that what you want?

OPUS MYSTERIUM

For what purpose is this fanatical and relentless stripping of normality, alongside a wholehearted devotion to Undead entities for, exactly? What does it truly mean when we write of things such as Lichood, evolution and Imperium?

The truth of such praxis, the black secret of our work is that we all, as acausal beings, can become so much more than the unending hordes of human cattle.

In the beginning, such devotion is necessary. We must bow before our masters; They must be encouraged to come forth to guide us, to test us. Only those who remain sane and whole following such Communion shall be fit to discover the dark knowledge which has lay, for thousands of years, just beyond the grasp of waking humanity.

Once you have learnt to greet the shadows as veritable brethren, and once you have lived and bled for Them, having achieved the completion of various physical tasks, and having spent countless nights among the graves of the dead, only then can you truly call yourself an adept. And only when you have pushed your body and mind beyond all limits can you truly be considered prepared to begin the bleak and lonely path toward our ultimate aim – a grand Apotheosis, to become free of the mortal shell in an explosive rite which claims hundreds if not thousands of causal lives, and which sees your acausal essence transformed, feeding on the plasma of endless stars, feeding on the Blood Essence of countless species scattered across the cosmos which we have not even begun to explore yet. And then in time, a return – either to this lowly sphere, or other, more primitive vistas, where your presence will be felt, and where you will in time be worshiped as a god – an entire planetary system devoted to you for this deed which you, Dark God, have fulfilled.

Live according to these tenets, to these unrelenting disciplines – and this shall be yours. This and much, much more...

THE MOOR

0

The somber playing of the clavichord echoed through the old house's walls, offering subtle tones to the chamber where Annalise dwelt, holding between her hands a crystal tetrahedron, greased with the blood from her hands.

Through the mist of dark sight given via her offering of blood induced by a sharp blade drawn across each palm, Annalise sent her presence to her newest acolyte, a young girl currently domiciled in a backwater village on the outskirts of Yorkshire.

Annalise had followed the Vampyric path, as laid out by her Master for over 10 years now. They had met when she was quite young, and he had given little, beyond a handful of teachings; but he, and what he had taught, had taken much from her. This cruelty was but a small price to pay, however, for the secrets Annalise learnt through his dark tutelage. The techniques of moving through the Acausal dimensions and feeding on the Blood Essence of myriads of victims, the secrets of the Dark Gods, the terrible rites – all had elevated far above she once thought she was.

With great power and wealth had come great burden, but greater joy. She had lost everything and gained everything. And now, her small army of minions acted as eyes and ears wherever she needed them; temple fronts, questionable enterprises and individuals, petty criminals with a lowly superstition (not difficult to find among the rural locales, and certainly not difficult to hold in sway with the abilities Annalise had slowly accumulated – physical and magickal).

Now, with a veritable foundation beneath her, she had set her sights higher. She knew the time was fast approaching to leave all this behind and undertake the Rite of Internal Adept. The Dark Gods demanded it. So few and far between were Their servants, and the Gates had to be opened.

Annalise now needed to find a suitable individual to govern in her stead. The few minions she kept close by were unreliable, and any semblance of order soon fell apart in the absence of her charismatic leadership. No, she would find one similar to herself and raise her through greatness so that she may have an heir.

Outside, rain began to fall lightly on the moor. The old house Annalise had acquired overlooked the countryside of Yorkshire on one side, and offered a view of the village of Sayersby below on the other. The house had been a lavish gift. Through her natural ability to manipulate men, she had acquired much for herself (not difficult given her beautiful looks and charm – what man could resist this raven haired, blue eyed witch?). Yet none of them remained. They had been bled dry, and cast aside.

Annalise had learnt cruelty was not only a necessity, but a stalwart companion.

Listening to the sound of raindrops, the evening faded into night. With nightfall came the fading away of all the so human notions of logic and rationality, as darkness took its brief reign across the country. The ancient denizens of the moors roamed the countryside, unseen, unheard.

Ga Wath Am, Annalise whispered, stirring the cold air between her lips and the bloodied crystal. And far away, over the bleak moors and forests, a young girl sat upright, softly aware of someone at the foot of her bed...

I

Twenty years ago, a young girl discovered a book left behind in an old book shop in Ilkley. The shopkeeper said a man had left it behind after purchasing several large tomes on local history. The man had left before the shopkeeper noticed it lying on his counter. Being a collector of books, he decided to add it to his collection, thinking it may make a pretty penny perhaps, in the future.

The book was an old leather bound thing, nothing remarkable, save for a strange symbol embossed crudely into its front cover. It appeared to be two winged skeletal figures, grasping a circular symbol, not unlike the pentagrams the young girl had seen frequented by the villains of the horror films she and her friends would watch well after hours despite her parent's warnings. This symbol however, was more complex and – the young girl thought – more intriguing, more redolent of something worth investigating further.

Unfortunately, the shop owner informed her the book, whilst elegant looking and certainly a good piece of décor for the place, was filled in unintelligible script, with a few illustrations which made little sense. The young girl flicked through the pages, admiring the calligraphy and bizarre detail.

This young girl however was sharply intelligent – to the point of sociopathic, some would say. She knew this book was a test – left behind for the right person to find and decipher. And she would decipher it. She asked how much the book was, the owner offering it to her for a fraction of the price, knowing she would soon tire of its novelty and pursue other, gentler pursuits suited to a young girl. The old book collector watched Annalise leave and skip across the cobbled streets, the old tome in her satchel bag which swung from her shoulder.

Three days later, the book collector died, of an apparent heart attack. The shop, left unattended and for sale, its contents in boxes, succumbed one night to a fire. The fire consumed every book and journal the old man had amassed over the years.

II

Alexander stood, shivering in the cold rainy October morning, waiting by a rural road outside Halifax. His coat and bag – containing but a few books, change of clothes and other items of interest – (including a skillfully cut piece of quartz in the shape of a tetrahedron) – were growing wetter by the minute. He had arrived at the rendezvous, as commanded via email by the shadowy organisation he had been corresponding with over the past four months. What lay in store for him, he did not know and he had to fight an overpowering urge to just leave, to go home. What if they didn't turn up? What if they did, but they were nutters, what if they kidnapped him and demanded a ransom?

This is pretty stupid, Alexander thought to himself. He was cold, wet and bored. The grey skies, casting a grim spectre across the hills and farmer's fields all around him was showing no sign of letting up its steady torrent.

'Fuck it,' Alexander muttered, cold and annoyed, and began to head back down the long and winding country road.

However, a pair of headlights could now be seen in the mist of rain coming toward him, down the isolated and hilly moorside road. The car pulled up beside him, black and expensive looking, and he opened the door and got in, the dry warmth a welcome greeting.

'I didn't think you were going to turn up,' said Alexander, noticing a figure sitting in the back seat as he bent down to look in.

'Get in, you must be quite cold,' said a charming and smooth woman's voice.

Alexander got in the car, and it sped away up the hill, away from the town's outskirts.

Removing his wet overcoat, Alexander extended a hand and introduced himself to the woman sitting next to him. She was strikingly good looking, to the point of being intimidating. Her black hair and crimson lips accentuated the pallor of her porcelain skin.

Alexander,' she said, 'we finally meet. Lucas has told me much about you. He thinks you show promise.'

'Thank you,' Alex replied, 'I have been very interested in what your – erm, your group has written. I want to be like Lucas. I want to prove myself and gain power.'

Annalise smiled at him, a smile which Alexander could not figure out was genuine or cynical.

'They all start out so eager, don't they Jeffery?'

The mute drive turned his head slightly, a gruff laugh emanating from under his bristly yet well-groomed beard.

'Where is it we're going?' Alexander asked, looking out across the damp moor through the rain specked window, starting to feel uneasy at his trust of complete strangers. He thought he would be meeting Lucas, not two strangers in some posh car. No worries, he had his knife on him, in case things got out of hand. It wouldn't be the first time he'd used it either, though of course that was in self-defense.

'To meet the others,' Annalise replied, 'we cannot share all our information with you until we have ascertained your potential and dedication. I believe Lucas told you of my home, up on the hill, at Sayersby-on-Morton?'

'Sayersby – yes, I've been there before, as a lad – with friends. We used to dare each other to go into the town. The kids where I lived all believed it was haunted. Silly really, as there are people who live there.'

'That is not such a silly belief at all, Alexander. Not in my opinion, at least,' replied Annalise.

The rest of the journey they spent in silence.

III

Leeds, 8:30 am. A group of masked and armed men were heading, via a large van replete with blackout windows, to a high end jeweler, with every intent to rob and kill everyone they came across. The gang had, for some time, subsisted on a network of rackets and other forms of illegal trade, which kept them well monied and far more organised than most enterprises which flourished amongst the dark underbelly of the city.

However, times were changing and serious money was being made by their rivals. The need for a massive cash influx had become necessary; an investment which could be turned into hard drugs and other items of continual worth. The gang had specialised, in their early days, at the brazen task of taking out drug dealers and other gangs – taking their merchandise and leaving them crippled beyond recognition. They thus built their reputation on cold hatred, but more importantly – cold fear. The criminal underworld was shaken by the ripples of such acts. Gangs turned upon one another, breaking uneasy alliances through paranoia. The more this shadowy organisation struck, the more the criminal system was brought to its knees. In time, they revealed themselves, leaving their calling cards here and there, upon a dead dealer or a burnt out car. The head, rumored to be among many things, an ex-special forces operative, a long time convict and more fancifully – a devil worshipper with a sadistic bent – had shown a ruthless tactic and strategy in destabilising the criminal elements, before building it back up in his image, reaping the rewards.

This had all been done under the watch of a paralyzed police force, who had seen nothing like this before. The deep rooted corruption in the institution was starting to come undone, and a few cash in hand off duty types were getting restless. They launched a bold plan to assist the previous criminal enterprises so as to act as a resource diversion and a convenient enemy to this new group, hoping to exhaust and wind them down, whilst also keeping the money flowing in their direction, lest their grubby hands be no longer crossed with notes from the underworld.

So now the gang was headed to Goldman's jewelers. The intent was twofold – to make a tidy sum to pump into an investment of various sorts, and to drive a message home to Louis Goldman, the Jewish city patron who was known to have hands in many illicit trades going on in the back rooms of the sleazy clubs he had built up on the fortune of his father's jeweler's shop. Nobody touched Goldman, and that was the reason they were headed there. This city would learn who its true masters were.

In the passenger seat sat Lucian, the gang's illustrious leader and mastermind. In his hands he held an object he treasured greatly – a small finger bone, inscribed with strange runic symbols. He often wore it around his neck, and claimed it was from a militia leader he had killed in Sierra Leone. The item was one of many macabre and unsettling things about Lucian, but he was a genius – and his boys knew it. He brought them riches, he called the shots. And they paid off big time.

They arrived at their destination, just as the manager and security guards were arriving and opening up. The men leapt out of the van, armed with their weapons – not the usual sawn off shotguns for them, but a collection of SMGs recently smuggled in from the coast. The men, all in black attire, swiftly surrounded the manager and guards, forcing them to their knees, one guard being knocked to the ground with a hard jab from a gun butt to the face, before being kicked to stillness by two other men. The manager was forced in, two barrels aimed at his head. 'Open the fucking safe or you die today,' barked one of the men, leading him on whilst the other six began gathering the jewelry from the shelves and display cabinets, smashing glass as they did so.

The raid was over in ten minutes and the van sped away into the outskirts of the city, sirens filling the morning air.

IV

The house loomed over the village of Sayersby-on-Morton, a bleak sentinel against the grey skies which shadowed the moorland. As the car pulled into the driveway, Alexander marvelled at the house's appearance. Whilst not a mansion in itself, it was old, and rather ominous – everything about the place spoke of dark intent. The door was opened by the driver, and Alexander and Annalise stepped out, she leading him into the house.

'This is very nice,' said Alexander, unsure what to make of the surroundings. It was decorated expensively, and there were a few portraits on the walls of presumably important, but unknown figures.

'Yes, we keep a good household running. This is our temple, and you will be staying here with us, on the first floor, second bedroom. Jeffrey shall show you to your room.'

Alexander dutifully followed, and leaving his bag by the door, sat on the bed, already made for him. He pulled his quartz tetrahedron out of his pocket, and held it in his hands, admiring its blemishes and polished faces.

Downstairs, Annalise sat by the fire, accompanied by a dark looking man in a neat suit. The light tapping of the rain upon the windows created a contrasting din to the crackling of the fire.

'So, I hear news that our wayward son has been causing havoc in the city?' she asked.

'Quite; nobody's been able to infiltrate them, and they've recently made a daylight robbery at Goldman's. They took off with a small fortune.'

'Hmmm, he is a wild one. What are your superiors planning to do about it?'

'Well at present, there's not much they can do, beyond circulating descriptions of the gang to the public. We've tried getting a few informers in, but nobody is risking it.'

Marcus was an investigative officer, a long serving member of the West Yorkshire police, and like most men in the temple, deeply in love with Annalise. His time in the force had been an insightful one, and one which he had chosen so as to gain experience, as was asked of his and Annalise's path. He had met her a handful of years ago, and she had found him to be of great use – a pair of eyes in high up establishment, trusted, reliable, ruthless.

'Well, perhaps I'll have to call him out myself,' Annalise responded, drifting toward the window, and petting the dark grey cat stretched out on it lazily. 'He has been involved too long to know his transgressions won't go unpunished. Stealing from me to fund his own upstart adventures was a stupid move. Something we shall have to make clear.'

'Understood ma'am,' Marcus responded. Conditioned into obedience by his police training made orders very easy for him to follow. Something Annalise utilised to brutal efficiency.

'The time is drawing near as it is; Wyrd has panned things out quite well. Young, an initiate – he is perfect for the opfer rite,' Annalise mused, gazing out of the window across the quiet village. Silhouetted against the bay windows, in a flowing crimson dress, her black hair nearly reaching her waist, Marcus felt a mix of adoration and frustration. She was a beautiful and calculating woman. He vowed to win her favour.

He left, without saying a word, driving his operative car down toward the village, and out across the moors – toward Leeds, where a steady rain was gathering over the city.

The priest who slew the slayer, and shall himself be slain, whispered Annalise, as Bedwyr brushed her hand with his fluffy tail, purring at her affections.

She rose gracefully, and headed toward her room, where she was to prepare for that evening's rite, a piece in a grand culmination of her plans to rid herself of an antagonist, and replace herself with an heir.

V

Siofra awoke, short of breath and heart pounding from the dream – the same dream she had been plagued with for several nights now. She was walking on a dark moor, toward a woman in a long red dress. The woman smiles, and extends her hand, before they both fall into blackness. She awakes in a small village, abandoned and overgrown with ivy, with a dark forest wrapped in mist in the distance. She has vague recollections of villagers telling her to avoid the forest, and despite not wanting to go to it, she feels impelled to do so. She approaches, with bats beginning to fly out from the trees. More keep flying toward her as she heads deeper into the forest, till a veritable cloud of them is circling a clearing, in which is a rough stone altar. The rocks crumble away and a pale creature – a woman with terrifying red eyes and bloody mouth emerges.

Siofra got out of bed, and showered, trying to escape the atmosphere of her nightmare, clinging to the edges of her mind. The water washed away her fogginess, and after she finished breakfast and was dressed, she headed out into the bright morning.

The town of Haworth was nice, but Siofra felt cramped. She felt truly alive out on the hills and the wilderness. The old cobblestones did always feel reassuring under her feet, as if time and modernity could not remove some things, some things always remained, and old was good in her mind.

From across the street, Lucas saw the girl Annalise had identified – the photo matched. How she had found this girl was anyone's guess, but Lucas had learnt not to question Annalise. She was rarely one to pursue cold leads.

Lucas approached Siofra, and struck up a conversation. She was shy and didn't seem too keen to engage with a complete stranger, but this young man was handsome and charming. She gave the directions he asked for and returned the smile.

'I'm Lucas by the way. I live in Sayersby, though my family are from Heptonstall.'

'I'm Siofra,' she replied curtly.

'Siofra, a lovely name. Will I see you again, do you think?' he asked, giving his best charming smile.

'I don't know – I do live here! You might do.'

'Well, if I do, I would like to buy you a drink sometime.'

'Is that so?' she replied. She was charmed and taken aback by his forthright attitude, but he seemed harmless enough.

Lucas and Siofra met again, via an engineering of events on his and Annalise's part, and as they got to know one another, she gradually opened up about her dreams, and her life of unusual experiences. She had grown up in Yorkshire, but her family were of Scottish descent. She had seen ghosts all her life, and had many unusual abilities. One event which confirmed her understanding of just how different, how essentially wyrd she was, was when her friends found a dead sparrow in the woods when they were children. She told Lucas how she held it in her hands, looking into its lifeless eyes, and breathed on it, not knowing why, but doing so anyway. The bird took to life, and flew from her hands as if it had woken from a stupor. Her friends were naturally shocked and from that day, she developed a reputation as a witch, what some of those old enough to remember the cunning folk of yesteryear called a Rounwytha.

Her life had thus been marked by odd occurrences, odd powers, and more recently, odd dreams. Lucas offered to introduce her to his family, though the way he used that word seemed different.

'We are part of a group – a coven, you could call it, though we're all close friends – we're family like I said.'

'Ha, like witches?' she asked, bemused.

'You'll see. I think you'll get on with them. Maybe you can meet them sometime.' Siofra liked Lucas, he was funny and witty, and so she agreed to meet Annalise, the woman who he claimed had been like a mother to him for some years now.

VI

Alexander was struggling to sleep. The house was deathly quiet, and the only sound which could be heard was the soft patter of rain which scattered across the moors on most nights – yet he couldn't drift off. The last few weeks certainly had been different to his normal day to day life.

Earlier that day, Annalise had taken him up on to the hills of the Yorkshire moors, to a ruined cairnstone. There she had shown him a stunning vista of the bleak landscape, and pointed out certain areas pertinent to her coven's tradition. She then reached into the cairnstone and pulled out a tattered leather-bound book which had been stuffed between two of the stones. She told him to read it and speak with her again back at the house once he had done

CODEX ARISTARCHUS

so. Alexander was then instructed to head down the hills toward the woods, where he would find a house at the edge of the tree line. He set off diligently, and Annalise soon faded from sight, her stark beauty accenuated by the wind which blew her raven black hair and dress against her lithe form atop the barren hill.

Alexander soon reached the woods, after much climbing down and trekking across uneven terrain. It had taken him just under an hour to reach it, and sure as Annalise said, he saw the abandoned house – a cottage, overgrown with ivy, its roof partially caved in and the windows grubby and back – those windows which did remain, of course.

Stepping through the doorless threshold, Alexander's eyes adjusted to the dark and he was greeted by a musty and dilapidated central living room. It was low roofed and cramped, with the walls lined with bookcases and other shelves now mostly bereft of belongings. Birds had settled on the roof beams, and thus there was a mess of hay and feathers here and there on the moss coated floor. In the centre of the room, where the wooden flooring was still somewhat intact, Alexander could make out a triangle of lines and sigils carved into the surface of the wood. He recognised one of them, and checked the leather journal Annalise had given him – the very same symbol adorned the leather cover.

Alexander sat upon the floor and read the journal.

He followed the instructions written in Annalise's flowing script, which demanded that he set up a brazier filled with moss and petrichor, along with a blend marked 'Nightbane'. He found these three ingredients in murky bottles laying on one of the shelves, as the journal said, and he blended them together, as Annalise had shown him previously in her greenhouse.

He then removed his tetrahedron from his backpack, and making an incision on his hand, he whispered *Agios O Wamphyri*, and placed both his hands upon it.

He sat there, in diligent meditation, practising the technique he had learnt, which Annalise had described as 'Lich breath', as the incense slowly filled his nostrils. The ground beneath him began to sway, as Alexander's vision dimmed. He felt himself becoming dizzy and nauseous, but he held still and continued his meditation.

In the corner of the room, where damp had grown up along the wall, there slowly developed a sickly, mucous shadow emanating and darkening the room in its hideous mire. Alexander turned toward it, his sight dizzied and his mind unsure of the reality of the situation.

Through the luminescence, the shape of a haggard old woman stepped through, her legs bowed, her back hunched and her form concealed by a ragged black cloak which covered her body. Alexander reeled from the stench and a ringing in his ears, as the hag drew nearer.

Suddenly, she was upon him, and he had to wrestle with all his might to keep from being restrained, as the fiend straddled him, her matted grey hair blinding his vision and her grey nails dug into his wrists. She laughed maniacally, and he felt the two of them spin around the room as if flying. The furniture and items upon the shelves flew around the small room with him, and Alexander strained to remain upright in this maelstrom of madness he now found himself within.

The old witch grabbed the back of his head with one hand and pressed the other to his mouth, forcing a few streams of her blood into his mouth. His throat was on fire, and still they kept flying around the cottage ruins, which had taken on unearthly dimensions and was now totally suffused with a dank stench of wet earth.

Alexander fell to the ground, and passed out.

VII

Lucas had introduced Siofra to Annalise soon after befriending her, and the three of them met in Leeds for lunch on a sunny Thursday afternoon. Annalise was, as always the charming host, and Siofra found that she felt at ease around her. This beautiful woman seemed very interested in what she had to say, and seemed to know about the night terrors and visions which had plagued her for some years now. Annalise in fact claimed they made

Siofra special, and that there were people who spent years trying to attain the visions she received. She relayed to her a story of peasant traditions and secret lineages, a fascinating history of the land as they enjoyed their lunch, and Annalise offered for Siofra to come stay with her and Lucas for a few days. There, she was promised, she would be made more than welcome and she could use Annalise's library to her heart's desire.

Siofra was soon ingratiated into the family, tentatively at first, till she was made aware of the covenant tradition and how it related to her own experiences and skills.

Then, one moonlit night, a couple of weeks after they had first met, Siofra was given a sacred infusion to drink by Annalise, and within one of the many dark rooms of the old house, the two of them made love.

Siofra was initiated that night – into the ways of Sapphic love by Annalise's adept fingers and tongue – and into the vampyric tradition, by the unseen entities, who bestowed a two-way gift of Blood Essence upon her once the two of them, satiated, collapsed from orgasmic exhaustion. Siofra fell asleep in Annalise's arms, who toyed with her wispy blonde hair and stroked her young porcelain skin with a steady hand. She whispered as Siofra, still light headed from the potion, drifted into sleep –

'Unto you I give everything I have built, just as he who came before me did so. A child you shall bear, and our lineage shall grow. But always will you contain the seed

of my Essence, and that child shall be ours, a new Sinister species., which in time shall rule this planet and haunt the stars...'

Alexander awoke, his mouth dry and his head aching. It was now twilight, and the abandoned cottage had grown dark. The light, the witch, the madness – all were gone. He stood up, feeling faint, and packed his belongings. He knew what had occurred and why it had to be as it was. He had been initiated by one of the Covenant's dead Masters, an elite of horrific entities who had achieved the blackest of powers during life and who had stepped across the threshold of Death as easily as he had into the cottage. Now they lurked, haunting their respective remote places, and making their dark presence known to those who served them.

It was nightfall when Alexander returned, and Annalise stood at the door, with Siofra by her side. The two of them created a curious contrast – Annalise, tall, dark and of indeterminate age; Siofra, petite, fair of hair and barely in her 17th year. Yet both of them were now aligned toward the same purpose, and Siofra now had within her that vampiric and acausal seed, which was slowly mutating her into something powerful and dangerous.

Annalise greeted Alexander with a clap of her hands and a sinister smile, and informed him that dinner was being served shortly. Alexander was understandably hungry, and headed inside to shower, eat and then dwell upon what had transpired that day. Meanwhile, Annalise had preparations to make, and she awaited the arrival of several – a dozen or so, perhaps – of her loyal followers, as they arrived to the meeting place deep in the trees just over the next hill.

Siofra departed her lover with a tender kiss, and proceeded to take dinner with Alexander and Lucas, with Jeffrey serving a delicious meal as was his custom and habit most nights.

VIII

The pine forest was shrouded in a thick darkness, the cold wind snaking its way through the trees which were nestled in a deep valley in the West Yorkshire moorside. A circle of small torches, pitched into the earth had been arranged, and upon the closest trees hung black banners, bearing archaic and sinister looking sigils. A circle of black clad men and women, outfitted in military grade clothing and boots, their faces obscured, were stood in silent attendance, as Annalise stood within the loose fire lit circle, hissing sibilantly, her arms raised and in which were held a tetrahedron. On either side of her were knelt two young girls, adorned like she, in flowing black robes which were decorated in unusual scripts and symbols. Each had upon their heads a headdress-cum-visor, which shielded their entire faces and locked them away from sensory input from the outside world. They were both equipped with parchment and pen, and were swaying subtly, intoxicated from the sacred herbs they had imbibed in a preparatory sapphic ritual prior to this event.

The circle of attendees each produced their forearm, as Annalise moved toward each one in turn, incising a small cut, which she bled into a wooden bowl she carried, before returning to the centre.

Binan ath ga wath am, Annalise slowly chanted and lowered the crystal into the bowl, bloodying it, its facets gleaming sickly in the fire light. The circle of black sentinels began to chant in unison, a chant hideous and crafted by the elders of their nexion:

Communio cum aliis Electissimus... Educet me in tenebris inpellentur

Lamia dei... tangunt me cum essentia... commune cum me

Lamia dei, commune cum me

As they chanted, a thick and cloying mire seemed to spread along the forest floor, and the two young girls, the Lamia Naturalae, became more alert and active, scrawling upon the parchments and wailing in strange tones. The circle of attendees knelt downward and continued to chant, in hushed tones now. Any further information the Ascended Masters chose to relay during this rite of sanctification was to be noted and pored over later by Annalise.

Annalise took the bowl and sipped the blood, liberal amounts of the crimson liquid soaking down her pale chin and throat, and offering it up to the unseen intelligences who were now relaying information through her twin mediums. She scattered the blood on the ground and around the circle with her fingers, before placing it on the ground in the centre. The two mediums had filled their parchments and had entered a frenzy, cackling and slashing their arms open and decorating the words scrawled in crimson.

'Ascended Masters, You who have guided our covenant for generations, hear me now! Your words are received, Your will shall be made manifest. Let all who offered their blood to You receive illumination in the darkest depths of night. May your black wings brush the faces of our nightmares. Let our deeds not go unnoticed – Lamia Dei, commune cum me!'

Two of the attendees came forward, carrying a small metallic box. They set it down before Annalise, who dipped a pen in the blood and inscribed a sigil upon the paper taped on top of the box, which was lined with rows of nails. The carefully prepared explosive device had been built by Lucas the night before, and now Annalise placed the quartz tetrahedron upon it, petitioning the unseen entities present to bless it, and to receive as a token of their loyalty all blood spilt upon its detonation. The bomb was ceremoniously wrapped, with the tetrahedron inside, and carried away by the attendees.

With the rite complete, Annalise sank to the ground, expended of energy, her mind swimming with external intrusions. She could feel Them circling her, feeding upon her, but in return, feeding her, imparting Their Undead Blood Essence and continuing to accelerate her evolution into something more acausal. The torches flickered, a few had gone out, and the forest settled into silence, the smell of frankincense wafting through the dark valley, as the rest of the world slept, oblivious to the black rites.

Later that night, back at the house upon the hill, which overlooked the quiet village now secluded in darkness, Annalise undressed in her bedroom, her pale skin covered by a fine silk nightdress and Japanese kimono gown. She lit a cone of incense on an altar in one corner of her room, a small and ornate mahogany table, on which was a grim altar, dedicated to her patron, the goddess Aosoth.

The parchment was laid on an oak table, covered in the dried blood and ink from the rite. Annalise sat and began to pore over the scrawlings, transferring them to a leatherbound notebook, and looking for symbols or words which stood out. She slowly deciphered a series of lines, numbers and what appeared to be a string of sentences. The words most closely matched a garbled form of gaelic of the Scottish variety. Translated, they spelt out what appeared to be a name or location – *Mor Beihnn Scithain*. The lines, when applied to a Scottish map, appeared to describe roadways, no longer there but clearly once present, as they ended at certain geographical points.

Annalise had much to discuss with the inner circle of her covenant.

She reclined into her bed, and dreamt the deep and obscure dreams which come from Communion.

Annalise stood on a barren and remote planet, its red sands giving way in the distance to sharp and jagged black shards the size of mountains. In the air hung four moons, the largest a sickly green hue. She had seen this place before, and knew its name – Mactoron. Before her stood a man, pale and handsome, ageless and sharp. The same man she had seen for many years since first finding his book in an old bookstore in Ilkley.

You have come so far Moraina Annalise. Your time to retreat draws near. Are you truly ready?

I am, Morain. And my heir is ready too.

Your name will live on for all eternity, till our people reach the sands of the planet we are now stood upon. I will not be so famed, but I will be felt. You will be a dark goddess, and we will grow powerful on the plasma of countless stars and the dreams of countless beings. All this is soon to be ours, Annalise. All we need now is aperiatur et terra germinet Atazoth!

With those words still ringing in her ears, Annalise felt herself flung billions of miles back to where she lay, and she awoke to a bright morning, the sound of birds singing outside.

IX

Allain was plotting. Through his informants in the police force, he'd heard how his former mistress and tutor was planning to move some serious merchandise in the dead of night along the Leeds canal, to a receiver in Liverpool. She had already proven herself to be a typical and shortsighted woman, easy to charm and get in to bed with the right words. Sure, she was smart – and had connections – but Allain was ruthless. His gang now owned the city; nothing went on without him hearing about it. The competition had been cut away ruthlessly, because he'd been patient and smart. And he had propitiated the Dark Gods. Surely he was living proof of Their power.

The gang was preparing in the abandoned factory outside Leeds which served as a drop off point, partial HQ and staging area for more occult operations Allain had become known for in his crew. Tonight, they would ambush Annalise's courier, and take the merch for themselves. Then, depending on the contents, they'd either hold it at ransom, or sell it on through the network of local fences. Now all he had to do was wait.

Allain toyed with his necklace, a finger bone inscribed with the sigil of Azanigin. He couldn't fail. His spy network never had yet.

It was 2:00 am in Leeds, and a lone figure stood by the canal which cut through the city. He was waiting for a small barge to drop the package off with, and with that, his deal would be done. He had been paid by a woman, known to a few of his crew who had dealings with her going back years. Though they were mostly all dead or locked up now, she had been vouched for. And the money was good, so why not?

The barge slowly and silently made its way down the icy black water, and the lone courier removed the contents from his satchel.

Suddenly, three men emerged from behind him, and before he knew what had occurred, the courier was shot in the head. The barge was fired at several times, and one of the masked men issued a warning, saying to send word to their men that 'she' would know who to contact to negotiate.

With that, the men sped off, jumping into a nearby car which had been parked nearby for a quick getaway.

Back at the established HQ, Allain watched as a car, its headlights blacked out, pulled into the waste ground surrounding the abandoned factory. His men emerged, bearing the package, and headed inside.

'Nice one lads, I knew I could count on you. Set it down on the table over there. Let's see what ol' Annalise is dealing these days shall we?'

One of the men opened up the package, and for a second there was silence. It was just a metal box, with some strange symbols drawn on it.

Their confusion however, quickly turned to panic as they heard sirens approaching, and before they knew it, several police vans had pulled up and surrounded the factory.

'Fuck! We've been ambushed!' shouted one of the men, moving to a window, gun drawn. Several armed officers were moving in.

Allain noticed the metal box was issuing a discernible sound, and he leant close to listen – ticking.

'Fuck.'

The factory was wracked by a terrific explosion, a fireball incinerating everything within its reach, debris scattered out across the waste ground and the surrounding street. Allain, his henchmen, and every surrounding police officer were charred to death in the immolating fire. From the centre of the smoldering carnage, an unseen figure emerged from a shard of shattered and burnt quartz, and eagerly fed upon the death and destruction wrought by Annalise's opfer rite.

Annalise was dreaming, or at least she thought she was. She stood next to her bed, watching her body lay next to Siofra's, the two of them blissfully wrapped in a warm bed. She felt a hunger, deep and ravenous and she turned toward the window, where she could see the lights of Sayersby below.

She found herself sailing across the moor, her form black and terrible. The night was alive, and all around her she sensed the presence of winged horrors, brothers and sisters in her vampiric lust.

Her shadow arched over the village, and she swooped down on batlike wings, entering through the window of one of the houses. There she found her prey, sleeping. She fed deeply, bathing in the Blood Essence which she tore forth from her powerless victims, and satiated, flew up into the night, ecstatic and joyful in her power. This would be the last time she fed upon the people of Sayersby, though her coven would continue to do so.

Full with the accumulated energy of her opfers, she settled back to her residence, and awoke in her bed, Siofra beside her, blissfully dreaming her deep, dark dreams.

X

A few more weeks, perhaps a month, and the coven had been structured accordingly, with all affairs set in motion. The men were to serve Siofra's will, and Siofra was to be guided toward Adeptship, to continue the mission of the coven as laid out by those who came before.

Annalise would guide her, in dreams and visions. But she was to leave, heading north, where she would attain isolation and live out the next 6 months in solitude. She would then emerge as an Internal Adept, and from there – Wyrd would guide her.

She had single handedly built a formidable temple of the Covenant out here in the bleak moors, and she would go on to become a veritable legend amongst the Covenant's various lodges and lone practitioners.

In time, her final rites would come, and she would enter the realm of the Ascended Masters, her visage haunting humankind forever, her wisdom passed on to those who knew how to commune with her.

But for now, she prepared, and bid goodbye to Marcus, Lucas, Alexander, and a teary Siofra, to whom she imparted one last kiss, and to whom she promised greatness, if she but learnt how to master the pain of this loss.

'All that is great is built upon sorrow, Siofra. Do not shed a single tear, for I shall be there each night to lay with you and guide you. And in time, we will be reunited, Wyrd willing.'

With those words, Annalise left, her car driven down the winding village road, into the misty distance.

The house was empty without her presence, and the moors looked somehow greyer, bereft of colour, as if the life blood of the land had been stolen away.

XII

Morain slept, slept the deep and steady sleep of an ageless wanderer. His mind, detached from his body which was safely concealed within a large sensory deprivation tank in a dank basement beneath an old ramshackle house, travelled the cosmos, flying from star to star, a sojourn amidst vast nebulae and galaxial remains.

His thin arms, crossed over his chest, were punctuated by various tubes, feeding vital nutrients and life sustaining fluids, as well as the unique life extending protein he had synthesised so many years ago with the help of his disciples.

Now he was safe within the Blood Tank, reserved only for the Masters of the covenant temple he had carved over the years, drenched in the blood and sweat of countless acolytes and servants. His black empire – now extended clandestinely across the globe – worked toward fulfilling his dark vision.

He had seen the surfaces of planets no human would ever see, drank deeply on the acausal essence of beings so alien to any form common to Earth. His astral essence had been felt by thousands of these alien beings, and his form would become the seed of countless folklores and legends of cultures myriads of worlds away from the corner of the Milky Way he called home.

But now, he stirred. It was time to return his focus toward more familiar ground.

Before the sarcophagus of Morain's Blood Tank, a hunched figure in tattered and aged clothing knelt, awaiting his Master's presence to be felt.

Agios O Wamphyri...

THE EXEATIC URBAN VAMPYR CLAN

A more extreme take on the notion of Dreccian living is that which the Drakon Covenant describes as 'roaming vampire clans', and which the Drakon Covenant had its genesis in (123yf, Yorkshire).

These clans are essentially urban gangs with a specific agenda, namely being the spread of Sinister memetics and utilising their experiences on the harsh edge of society as a brutal pathei mathos, from which they can draw upon to engender a very real Vampyric Metamorphosis.

Like any mundane gang, the strictest of codes apply, and anything is for the taking. Experiencing life on the other side of the law, as a fully-fledged criminal – but one imbued with a Baeldrecan understanding of WHY you are doing what you are doing – is perhaps one of the most terrifying manifestations (from a mundane perspective) of the Sinister-Vampyric convergence.

Many urban regions, cities in particular, contain ample opportunity for criminal avenues of vampyric metamorphosis, and it is the accumulated pathei mathos of the Drakon Covenant that this essay will draw upon and attempt to outline so as to guide novitiates in the black path of alchemical evolution.

The cities of Man are Magian mentality centres, hubs of hedonism personified. Bustling by day with drones eager to make money, they come alive at night with the same drones eager to breed and spend the money they make. It is into this arena that the Vampyr enters, and thus we descend to explore this dual world.

The nightclubs, bars, the places where people gather and denude themselves of their senses are perfect hunting grounds. This is not for the petty practise of 'psychic vampirism' but for actual Exeatic praxis. You should be indulging in everything these cities have to offer – sex, violence (especially violence), drugs, and the whole cornucopia of this rotting edifice.

Throughout your explorations, or perhaps already, you shall discover others – criminals or pliable individuals who can be shaped into useful tools to serve you. Whether you initiate them into the unique ways of the Drecc is your own doing, but a code is always useful to follow. Whether you illuminate them on the vampyric aspect of this pursuit is another matter entirely.

Among the delinquent youth sectors which often coalesce in urban areas, you may find useful acolytes. This is a practise already utilised to efficiency, and provides a whole spectrum of illicit and forbidden pursuits for you to indulge in, as well as serve as a constant pool of recruitment.

Persuading these acolytes and setting up a useful enterprise within this sphere of influence is as easy as obtaining materials from the 'deep web' and profiting thereof. How you actually do this is all down to your self–

reliance and ability. How much are you willing to take to achieve your black Will?

Of course, others seek to profit amidst the nest of mundanes, and to this extent the body must be made hard – through physical trials designed to make one a living embodiment of Vampyric terror.

A useful step to take is to establish a headquarters. One's abode may serve well, but if pursuing criminal activities, such a choice would be unwise. No doubt the reader can discern what is meant here. The author acquired a collection of abandoned buildings surrounding the outskirts of a large city in Yorkshire for his exeatic pursuits. Those knowledgeable will see these places, and will recognise the symbols of the Dark Gods carved upon them. It will also be noted that these are the very same locales as detailed in the ONA MS 'Eulalia', concerning a particular scene.

It is well known that the causing of pain and suffering, through bondage and torture is a sure-fire way to extract the Blood Essence of an individual, and thus a secluded HQ and an army of thralls is always a useful thing to possess. Because you are going to make enemies, living as you do. And you are going to destroy them all, and turn them into your food source.

You should strive to live by the 21 Satanic Points, as detailed in Codex Saerus. Another useful motto you should take to heart would be this: one must have chaos in one's heart to give birth to a dancing star.

One must create chaos to evolve through.

Feed, Baeldreca

THE ALCHEMY OF HATE

In all hearts there is a source of hatred. It stems from anything; a person, a situation. This hatred should be recognised as a gift, a tool with which to immolate one's self and bring about rebirth via Vampyric metamorphosis. Hate is a tool with which to overcome. Hate is simply an intense desire to modify a phenomenon or situation, and striving to change this is natural, it is healthy.

The mundanes confuse hate for impotent frustration. They thus claim hate is unhealthy, to be let go of. Do not listen to such Nazarene propaganda. Wrath is the providence of God in their paradigm, and what is the Vampyr but a grim god? Focus on the object of your hate and strive to do something about it. Push your will to its utmost limits, and learn about yourself. There is nothing you cannot do if you apply your mind. This is the knowledge of the Black Adept.

Befriend your hatred and rebirth yourself as an agent of Evil, for what is evil but delighting in the suffering of those weak worms who have created a world where hatred has consumed you? What is Evil but the desire to delve into the most hidden, most forbidden places to find what no man ever has?

CODEX ARISTARCHUS

"The greatest epochs of our lives occur when we gain the courage to rechristen what is evil in us as what is best."

–Friederich Nietzsche

TENDRILS

Alexander sat by the window of the train, idly watching the fields and hills of the Calderdale countryside pass by to the soundtrack of the monotone engine and tracks below. The sun dappled meadows and trees were always a replenishing sight, especially on a morning as crisp as this.

Eventually the train slowed its pace, as it pulled into Bradford Interchange, allowing a steady stream of people onto its carriages.

A well-dressed man, in a sharp suit and briefcase sat down opposite Alexander, his neatly ironed shirt and designer tie sure signs of his material comfort. Alexander sensed his chance.

The man was engrossed in the daily newspaper as Alexander locked his eyes onto his target, and began to breathe steadily, visualising the Wamphyric Tendril, as taught by the temple, extend from his solar plexus and eyes, and snake toward the seated man. Alexander focused on the man's energy body, tearing it open and puncturing the energy centres, allowing sweet Blood Essence to seep forth. He plunged the tendril deeper, and drank of the core essence.

The victim, besides a slight shift and look of temporary discomfort, noticed nothing, though Alexander could be sure the man would, in a few days, feel the effects manifest in illness or persistent night terrors.

Alexander smiled, invigorated with a subtle mania which often accompanied such feeding. His eyes felt charged, almost glazed over. Such feeding ensured a steady increase in his powers, not to mention the attention of his ascended masters.

Twenty minutes later, the train soon pulled into Leeds Station, and Alexander departed. Behind him, a crowd had gathered around a man who had collapsed, clutching his chest – dead of an apparent heart attack.

LAMIA DEI,
COMMUNE CUM ME

On the attic floor of a quiet and dilapidated house, nestled in the corner of a damp, leafy English street, a man kneels bloodied, before a hideous sigil painted in his own blood upon a parchment before him.

The only light comes from an above light fixture, the original long ago replaced with a harsh red bulb and covered in a translucent black cloth, adding a Sinister crimson tint to the room, already darkened via large black out candles.

The walls are covered in sketching of bizarre alien entities, images and glimpses of long dead horrors attained during the quiet hours of sleep – entities which punctured through the lone individual's dream hours with the acute ferocity of wild beasts, bringing horrific knowledge, whether asked for or not.

In the corner of the room stands a dusty gramophone, a crackling vinyl playing an endless rendition of *Tiptoe Through the Tulips* via repeat, adding an unnerving dissonance to the bloodied and hushed scene, and serving to induce a not altogether welcome level of mania within the individual's mind.

The lone figure is covered in cuts and bruises, thanks to the fanatic administration of a crude metallic flogger, which he is repetitively striking himself with, sending light drops of blood onto the walls around him, adding to the already claret stained sketches of eyeless Horror, the only witnesses to his heresy this night.

A low and monotone chant is escaping from his lips, a chant crafted to highlight the attention of Those who may be watching this act of Sinister devotion.

Upon the parchment, on which is drawn a sigil – revealed in dream via Undead auspices – sits a tetrahedron of quartz, crusted with previous layers of blood, attesting to the repetition of this grisly Rite over the last three days.

The air in the room has slowly grown staler, colder; somewhat more charged. The smell of petrichor begins to entice the flagellant's nostrils. He knows They are coming.

Upon the wall opposite him, a veined darkness begins to grow like damp, crawling steadily up to the ceiling. With it, his consciousness fades, and he feels his body become more detached and swiftly numb. The lone figure looks down, seeing this body laid in a hunched position due to his knelt posture, his back exposed, and he sees now the strikes and damage caused by his favourite implement, christened in his blood and named – Azanigin.

Discarnate from his physical shell, the lone figure looks toward the wall and sees three shadowy entities, silently watching him. Their tattered robes and skeletal frames show no hint of humanity. They ooze the very feeling of dread – something not unnoticed by the lone figure, who is now gripped with a very real and terrifying paralysis. The centre figure, whose hood comes to a large and regal point, and who is dramatically taller than his two attendants, extends a lithe claw and draws our protagonist close, the breath of this ageless entity a repulsive and sickly stench. There begins a loud and constant drone, akin to radio static and the figure who has called these Ascended Masters to him begins to black out, fading away into oblivion.

When he awakens, he does so, drained and anaemic. His hand is clutching a pen and the parchment in front of him is covered in scrawlings. He slowly reads the writings, wiping away the congealed blood.

Three words are written in a language he does not understand. The record has stopped playing. The light has died, and it is morning.

A soft wind scatters the fallen leaves across the steps of the old house.

ANARCHAEON – A BRIEF LOOK AT THE FUTURE

The world which we, the inner sanctum of the Drakon Covenant prophesise and which our elite footsoldiers of the Vampyric Front work toward tirelessly is one of true terror and of true awe.

The world we see is slowly decaying, a state all those wise enough to recognise foresaw so long ago. The world continues, despite the smug 'statistics' of the liberal, Magian zombies, to break into smaller regions, characterised by tribal conflict; the megalopolis that is America is grinding to a halt. Europe is inflamed with religious and racial terrorism. Soon, the world will return to barbarism, and the Dark Age which will ensue shall purge the world of its hubris which it has accumulated, and for which it is now suffering.

Into this blasted and charred arena, will we see a return to primitive ways of thinking, the return of superstition, the death of reason – the return of Them. Once more will the world be plagued by acausal horrors by night, and by day, trampled underfoot by the relentless ranks of the servants of the Ascended Masters.

Even now, as you busy yourself and move among the crowds of thousands, of millions of humans, They gather and wait. They are making their presence felt, as evidenced by the exponential increase in the belief of

CODEX ARISTARCHUS

demons, ghosts, and more recently 'shadow people'. All this is occurring in spite of the supposed continuation in scientific understanding and discovery.

Why is this? Why are millions of people choosing to believe in such things? Why are millions of people seeing such entities? Why are millions of people finding themselves preyed upon each time they go to sleep at night?

The gates are opening, the acausal is drawing nearer – whether due to the increase in adepts and nexions functioning, or as part of some Cosmic cycle, it is irrelevant. What matters is that They are getting closer, and They are making Their presence felt in a very real way.

By aligning yourself with the inevitable, you become one of the Elite, who will master the arts laid out according to the Black Lodge in general, and the Drakon Covenant in particular. In time, you will be given the chance to ascend and sit among the ranks of the Undead. And from your vantage point, immortal and omniscient, you will be hailed as a god over the coming Anarchaeon, the Dark Age which humanity is hubristically hurtling toward.

We foresee a future ruled over by sprawling black empires, an unbreakable chain of caste, beginning with the lowliest slaves and terminating in the higher echelons of the Master Elite and the Ascended Undead whom they serve and with whom they will hold communion.

For the slightly less lucky, tribalism will return – as is Man's natural state. And these mundanes will have to learn to make friends with Nature once again, a terrible force they have smugly believed they were exempt from, a force which will shock them into very real awakening.

And when they tire of such an awakening, when the terror of the new world is too much to bear and they turn to rest, perchance to sleep – WE will be there, to feed eternally.

You are flanked by black clad soldiers, masked and bearing breathing apparatus to counter the toxic clouds which permeate the land you are moving through. The soldiers, your personal retinue, are armed with vicious and highly customised M4A1s, scopes and bayonets equipped as standard.

Around you is the wreckage of what was once called civilisation, now ground down to piles of corpses and burnt out vehicles. Black, oily clouds of burning plastic billow across the cracked pavements and roads, and the only light illuminating the night is from various fires smouldering in the distance.

As your retinue sweeps forward in tactical formation, you, an Elite adept of dread countenance, robed entirely in black, follow suit, heading toward your destination. The silence is punctuated by controlled bursts from the soldier's guns as they ruthlessly put down the few savages who emerge from the rubble to investigate this grim spectacle passing through their territory.

You possess abilities the other soldiers do not, and beside the litter of the post-apocalyptic landscape, you see other more nebulous forms, hulking across the wastes or streaming down from the sky in great tendril-like forms, winged and ribbed in horrific fashion.

You are heading toward the shell of the inner city, which looms over the charred horizon. The sides of the crumbled towers and apartment buildings are lit orange by the many fires flickering in the night, giving the impression of a gaunt and tattered sentinel, towering over the land.

Above you, the cold void of space hangs, punctuated by a myriad of stars, seen through the red hue that tints the horizon whichever way you look. Some points of light gleam brighter than others, and you feel a connection with these, as you recall the entities which call such stars home and sustenance alike. It is to these which you, the adept aspire to become and be worshiped in kind upon mortal termination by other adepts belonging to the cult you ruthlessly have carved into the fabric of this new world.

What was once simply myth and legend is now terrifying reality. Darkness, chaos, murder, discipline – all are necessities, cleansing the DNA of Man and rebuilding him into something purer, something which your dark vision has foreseen, and which They who watch from above have commanded.

Amidst the ruins of the city, you make your way across tumbled pillars and car-filled trenches, creating an uneven pathway spattered with potholes and ditches, of which various wild animals bolt from upon your approach. Rats, in their hundreds stream from underneath cars, incredulous to your presence and pausing here and there to gnaw on the desiccated skeletal remains which hang out of the vehicles so haphazardly arrayed. Rotting corpses, testament to long passed violence and anarchy of unprecedented levels hang from the overarching streetlights, their slack jawed grimaces and hollow eye sockets staring down upon you, swaying slightly in the breeze.

A pack of feral dogs approaches, but are easily scattered by short controlled gunfire from two of the soldiers.

You look about, seeing the imprints of the civilisation around you, seeing patterns and structures now long faded from the causal world, but lingering still in the astral, which you are able to glimpse into for a time. All this will in time be reduced to dust, and a new empire will take its place – one far more ambitious and promethean in its scope.

Eventually, you arrive at an intersection, where various main roads meet, cluttered with rows of cars and vehicles. Ahead lies a monolithic building, relatively intact in comparison to the surrounding towers, made out of steel and glass as opposed to this building, carved from stone of an enduring quality.

You ascend the steps which mark the entrance to the grand edifice, its steps strewn with corpses and bullet shells. The doors are wide open, long ago blasted by insurgents attempting an attack on whomever dwelt within.

The large building is a library, a central hub of knowledge in the once sprawling metropolis you find yourself and your guard within.

Making your way through piles of paper and ruined books, you find a tome, leather-bound and crumpled – the book you have been looking for. Stashed between other tattered volumes, you pull it out and see it printed in large and plain letters – THE SINISTER TRADITION.

Left here long ago by a wandering traveller who had no time for superstition, he had chanced upon it lying by the roadside and intended to keep it for kindling. Upon reaching the library, the wanderer had found more suitable material, and so placed the damp book on a shelf, forgetting about.

That was until this wanderer passed through your settlement and mentioned offhandedly to a fellow drinker what he had seen. This chance remark had been picked up by one of your many acolytes, and following a swift interrogation, the co-ordinates of the city remnants and been scouted and located.

You now possessed another valuable artefact to add to the growing collection of a select genre of literature, for which you could peruse and discover more secrets pertaining to the Dark Gods – and with it, more power.

They are watching. Their black hand is upon you. The taint of the Undead has forever now stained you.

www.ingramcontent.com/pod-product-compliance
Lightning Source LLC
Chambersburg PA
CBHW070615050426
42450CB00011B/3065